Pursuing Clara

Researching the mysterious, improbable life of a Granville Ferry girl

Ernest J. Dick

© 2020 Ernest J. Dick

All rights reserved. No part of this book may be reproduced or transmitted in any form or by any means, electronic or mechanical, including photocopying, or by any information storage or retrieval system, without permission in writing from the publisher.

Cover: Rebekah Wetmore
Clara Sabean portrait enhanced by Melissa Fillmore, Past to Present Photos
Author photo: Robert Albota
Editor: Andrew Wetmore

ISBN: 978-1-7772937-0-3
First edition October, 2020

397 Parker Mountain Road
Granville Ferry NS
B0S 1A0

moosehousepress.com
info@moosehousepress.com

We live and work in Mi'kma'ki, the ancestral and unceded territory of the Mi'kmaq People. This territory is covered by the "Treaties of Peace and Friendship" which Mi'kmaq and Wolastoqiyik (Maliseet) People first signed with the British Crown in 1725. The treaties did not deal with surrender of lands and resources but in fact recognized Mi'kmaq and Wolastoqiyik (Maliseet) title and established the rules for what was to be an ongoing relationship between nations. We are all Treaty people.

Other Ernest J. Dick books

Remembering Singalong Jubilee: The story of the CBC show that launched East Coast music

Voices from a Forgotten Tragedy: Trans-Canada Air Lines Flight 831

Silver Hair and Golden Voice: Austin Willis from Halifax to Hollywood

Being the Song: Vic Mullen from Clare to Nashville to Preeceville, Saskatchewan is in the works!

Acknowledgements

Jim How is the inspiration and example for my involvement with the heritage of the Annapolis Basin. He was an old friend of Nancy's family from his days as historical guide at the Habitation at Port Royal, and pioneered living with the past at Fortress Louisbourg for Parks Canada and then at the deGannes-Cosby house in Annapolis Royal. Jim knew Charlotte Perkins and encouraged me to have my way with 'Lottie', his Sunday School teacher.

Jim's virtual conversation with Charlotte Perkins about our history remains available as a Virtual Museum of Canada website.[1]

Jim How knew nothing of Clara, thereby emboldening me in my becoming historical detective pursuing Clara.

Women competing and performing in water were ignored until British historian Dave Day took notice of the Beckwiths, the first family of swimming. Professor Day has been most helpful to my research. Dave's evaluation and analysis of 19th century identity theft is included here, with permission, as an appendix. His understanding of the Beckwiths within their British context has been most valuable and is heartily recommended.

British writer Caitlin Davies' novel *Daisy Belle: Swimming Champion of the World*, imagining Clara's older sister Agnes Beckwith, is great fun. Thank you for Daisy Belle and your generous reading of *Pursuing Clara*. I hope these two ladies can meet somehow in the 21st century.

Friends and family were both helpful and wary of my pursuing Clara. A copy of *Pursuing Clara* is waiting for Donna Lee Butler, Tanya Dawson, Bob Dunfield, John Kirby, Lois Jenkins, Ian Lawrence, Ken Maher, Alan Melanson, David McClafferty, Rion Microys Wayne Morgan, Barry Moody, Doug Parker, Ruth Ritchie, Denise Rice, Ryan Scranton, Frank Taylor, Donnie Theriault, Kent Thompson and Deb Wade at "Mad Hatter Books" in Annapolis Royal. Over my ten years plus of this project I have completely forgotten who brought me which lead—and thus attribute all of their contributions to **George**, my favourite father-in-law.

I also need to acknowledge librarians from Saint Mary's University to our local Annapolis Valley Regional Library branch—even if I often never knew their names (and hence call them all **Libby**). Librarians are the most helpful and non-judgmental people on the face of the earth and it has been a great pleasure to work with them and alongside them for my career.

Tanya Dawson brought great energy to pursuing Clara. Tanya is a dedicated genealogist, a paralegal researcher—and a relative of Clara's. She stumbled onto Charlotte Perkins' story of Clara when she began her own family history in 2012. Clara's father and Tanya's 3rd great-grandfather were brothers, making Clara Tanya's first cousin, four times removed. Finding a relative was both hazardous and a great advantage to my project. Families can be very protective of their histories, even over many generations, but they also have intuition which may be as useful as forensic science. Tanya never exercised a protective prerogative over her long-lost cousin, and did access the probate records that allowed me to track Clara well beyond what Charlotte Perkins told us.

My great friend John Kirby has no hesitation or difficulty in imagining the past. He brought Mack Sennett and Bing Crosby to life on the stage at King's Theatre. John scripted the stories told by the ghosts of the Sinclair Inn in Annapolis Royal and the Perkins family at the Perkins House in Liverpool, Nova Scotia. John listened long (and read often) my speculations about Clara's accomplishments, wanderings, and re-inventions—and I always need that ear.

Finally, of course, I owe Moose House Publications a great debt in publishing this historical detective project. Andrew Wetmore is a patient and accomplished editor and the complications of 'pursuing Clara' over 10 years plus called on every bit of his empathy.

The Annapolis Heritage Society (based at the O'Dell House on lower St. George Street in Annapolis Royal) brings all of us together, whether we realize it or not. Thus any royalties *Pursuing Clara* may earn will be directed here. Clara's story is not finished, so do give me a call when that scrapbook of Clara's life shows up at a yard-sale or on the step of the O'Dell House.

Ern Dick,
Granville Ferry, Nova Scotia
August, 2020

Pursuing Clara can only be dedicated to Nancy, my life-partner and best friend for 49 years, who often had answers for the questions I was asking of anyone and everyone.

Notes on the text

There are a number of reference numbers throughout the text. The notes they refer to appear in the 'Notes' section at the end of the book.

The essay by Dr. David Day in the appendix appears with his permission.

The text of *In the Swim*, in the appendix, is based on the out-of-copyright version in the United States Library of Congress. After we secured that text, another publisher began offering for sale another, copyrighted, version of *In the Swim*. The text and images of *In the Swim* in this book bear no relation to any material in this newer publication, and instead draw on material in the public domain.

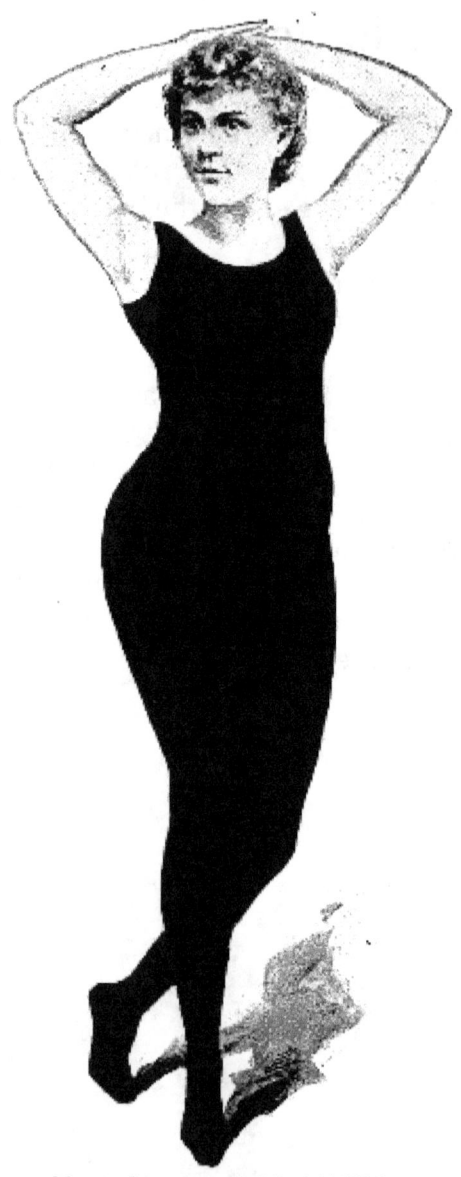

Figure 1: Clara, in her 'autobiography'

Table of contents

Acknowledgements..4
Notes on the text..9
Illustrations...12
1: Who, Where, What, When, How and Why?......13
2: Clara Sabean..21
3: Clara Beckwith...33
4: Mrs. Stanley McInnis..65
5: C. M. McInnis...71
6: Mr. Clement Miller...83
7: Clara Miller..89
8: Pursuing Clara..99
Afterword...109
Appendix A: *In the Swim*....................................113
Appendix B: Extract from *The Romance of Old Annapolis Royal*..169
Appendix C: From 1860s Lambeth to Niagara in the 1900s: Imitation and Innovation amongst Female Natationists...175
Appendix D: Timeline..197
About the author..240
Notes..241

Illustrations

Figure 1: Clara, in her 'autobiography'......................10
Figure 2: Agnes Beckwith..35
Figure 3: Mrs. Stanley McInnis.......................................64
Figure 4: The cover of Clara's 'autobiography'......113
Figure 5: The Chest Stroke...120
Figure 6: No time could be lost....................................126
Figure 7: Swimming on the Back.................................141
Figure 8: Floating...142
Figure 9: Diving, or Taking a Header..........................144
Figure 10: The Overhand Stroke.................................146
Figure 11: The Side Stroke...148
Figure 12: Swimming Without Using the Arms......149
Figure 13: Swimming Under Water...........................152
Figure 14: Treading Water...153
Figure 15: Beckwith Walking on her Hands...........155
Figure 16: The Old Post Office.....................................169
Figure 17: Ern Dick at the CBC....................................240

1: Who, Where, What, When, How and Why?

Clara Sabean was born in the Annapolis Valley of Nova Scotia in 1870. Clara, somehow, became **Clara Beckwith**, swimmer and performer extraordinaire in the 1890s in New England. She ran away from home on the steamer 'Hunter' and became "a water queen and living goddess" at the 'Boston Grand Museum' in the winter of 1888-9.

After competing and performing in the water and promoting swimming for some seven years, Clara went further away as **Mrs. Stanley McInnis** (wife of a successful dentist, thespian and legislator) in Brandon, Manitoba.

When Stanley McInnis died, endowing Clara with a life-long annuity, she quickly married **Clement Miller**, a musician in Boston—but came back to Annapolis Royal to open a hotel in 1909 as **C. M. McInnis**.

Throughout her adult life she was linked with Theodore Tebbetts from Lynn, Massachusetts, a wealthy industrialist, anglophile and 'Son of the Revolution' (a hereditary society perpetuating the men who achieved American independence from Great Britain), and was perhaps even responsible for him committing suicide in 1920.

Clara lived to 1943, spending the last dozen years of her life in the care of Boston Public Welfare, despite having substantial resources.

My 'pursuing Clara' has been organized somewhat chronologically following the identities she took on over her 73 years. I hope that organizing the chapters along these lines will help the reader follow her complicated life. Also, I had to use my high school history teacher's timeline to help organize Clara's stories, and offer this as an appendix to help the reader follow all of Clara's adventures.

I first stumbled across some hints of Clara's unlikely story thanks to Charlotte Perkins, the late Victorian chronicler of the history of Annapolis Royal, and include in the Appendix a passage from her book related to Clara. Charlotte was publishing, promoting, presenting and speaking about our history until she died in 1964. Her *Romance of Old Annapolis Royal* in 1924 introduced Clara's story and gave Clara as much space as Perkins accorded to the founders of New France or our Fathers of Confederation.

After all of these years it is impossible to remember who helped with which particular lead, so I acknowledge them collectively, in attributing them to **George**, my father-in-law. George Parker died long before I began this project and certainly would have been dubious about my interest in Clara, but I am sure would have been generous with his opinions, his liquor, and his unpredictability. He welcomed me into his family and his politics, though was always wary of my Upper Canadian superiority. George, in all of his incarnations and moods, became the perfect ally and skeptic in my 'pursuing Clara'.

I was regaling a local, aspiring actress with Charlotte's strange story of Clara, and got some detail of Clara wrong. George quietly, but decisively, corrected me. A great advantage of coming from away and wanting to be a Maritimer is that you get corrected a lot. You learn a lot that way. A disadvantage of coming from away is that you think you know better, when there is always more to learn

George's dismissing and denouncing of Charlotte's story of Clara undoubtedly would have prevailed without the advent of digital communications. One idle day I entered Clara's swimming name, 'Clara Beckwith', and 'swimmer' into Google and found 245 references. I checked them out. They showed that Charlotte Perkins had been more correct than either George or I had ever imagined.

Many references also led to dead ends or confusion, and I learned lots about the World Wide Web in my 'pursuing Clara'.

Libby often came to the rescue. Libby stands in for all the archivists and librarians too numerous to name. They are always patient, always interested in a patron's query—and I fell in love with each and every one who helped along my way.

George had no use for sports or athletic endeavours, one reason I was curious to know more about Clara. Many might be intrigued by Clara becoming the performer, but I was equally determined to take her swimming seriously. I have always considered physical challenges, be they gardening, hiking or sports, as metaphors for life, and 'pursuing Clara' was an opportunity to explore this further.

Clara was intriguing precisely because no one knew or cared about her. I have long been more interested in the untraveled paths than celebrated stories. I was an archivist rather than historian in my profession, because I was invariably distracted by all the stories the past had to tell. Here I became historical detective on Clara's behalf putting to good use all those mysteries I have read and all the cop and lawyer shows I have watched.

Clara had no remaining family or anyone else to protect her standing. More than once in my career I have run afoul of the hazards of fiercely asserted ownership of history, and no longer have the fortitude for challenging it. Clara's implausible and unknown story was thus fertile ground for me and, I hope, I do not become possessive and protective of 'my' Clara. But we will have to wait and see.

Finally, I will admit to having a thing for the ladies of the Annapolis Valley going down the road. Maritimers going down the road and coming back home have energized the world, themselves and the Maritimes by so doing, and following Clara affords me another way to know this story.

My life-partner, Nancy, had gone down the road and found me in deepest southwestern Ontario. She invited me back to Nova Scotia (where we eventually stayed) and was only a little jealous of my bringing Clara home.

Clara continuously re-invented herself (or was being reinvented), leaving scattered and intriguing clues, and died in Boston at the age of 73. I followed Clara from Nova Scotia, to New England, to Brandon and briefly back to Nova Scotia. She lived most of her life in Boston, with a few years in California, and did have an affinity for Baltimore. I followed whatever clues Clara inadvertently left me, but never did find the statue of Clara as "the most perfectly formed body in the world."

Then Clara, inexplicably, had an 'autobiography', *In the Swim*, which was published in 1893 when she was only 23! None of the other swimmers of her generation had anything similar. Obviously it was promotional, inventing a British Beckwith family legacy for Clara, and was perhaps written *for* her, rather than *by* her.

I found *In the Swim* in the United States Library of Congress website and pushed it onto George, Libby and anyone else who dared show any interest in my projects. I was eventually able to confirm the veracity of more of it than I expected. The full text and illustrations are in the Appendix. I do consider that Clara collaborated in its creation and believed in it.

George continued his skepticism of Clara's 'autobiography', and confirmation of anything therein is indeed problematic. It includes no dates, aside from her 26th of October, 1867 date of birth, which makes Clara three years older than she actually was. But then Clara always was very flexible with the year of her birth in all records throughout her lifetime, though never forgetting the actual month of October. This afforded me my first small clue as to the potential reliability of *In the Swim*.

Well beyond my archival training, George had been the one to show me how to look at a historical source many times, from different perspectives. He would bring a historical photograph to his nose, or hold it at arm's length, even upside-down or backwards, somehow finding clues that others had missed. Doing the same with Clara's autobiography, I eventually spotted her invented father as 'William Manning Beckwith', combining the name of a younger British Beckwith brother with that of her actual father, James/Joshua Manning Sabean, rather than 'Frederick', the famous patriarch of everything Beckwith. This was such a conspicuous and careful invention in light of everything else the 'autobiography' claimed correctly regarding the Beckwiths that it had to be taken seriously. Even George begrudgingly admitted that maybe I was on to something.

Pursing Clara happened because of the digital communications of the 21st century. I found dozens of ways to ask different questions of Clara and spent more than a decade, off and on, researching Clara from the comfort of my Granville Ferry home that overlooks the Annapolis Basin—exactly where Clara would have done her first swimming.

My research led me to Professor Dave Day, sports historian at Manchester University in the United Kingdom, who assured me that our local Clara was no Beckwith, despite her convincing claims in her 'autobiography'. Indeed, my Clara had wasted much of his time as she yielded more hits than did his Agnes Beckwith. He encouraged me in my research, and has made use of it in an essay about female natationists which you can find beginning on page 175.

My final chapter dares to offer my understanding of Clara. What motivated her? Who inspired, invented, controlled, or manipulated Clara? Who was Clara in Annapolis Royal, in New England, in Brandon and when she died at the age of 73 on public welfare? I will move from being the conscientious archivist and researcher, and finally become the historical detective 'solving' my pursuit of Clara and 'imagining' Clara.

2: Clara Sabean

Clara began life in the modest circumstances of rural Nova Scotia in the 1870s. Her mother, Abigail Jane Wade, was from Granville, which includes Port Wade on the Annapolis Basin. Her father, James/Joshua Manning Sabean, was from Port Lorne on the Bay of Fundy, though the Sabeans were often found in and around Clarence in the Annapolis Valley. The Wades were invariably enterprising folk whereas the Sabeans were hard-working quieter types.

Jane and Manning were married on the 22nd of August, 1868 in Parker's Cove Baptist Church, across the Annapolis River and the North Mountain from Annapolis Royal. Clara's birth in October of 1870 was registered at Paradise or Wilmot, perhaps because the parents were living there at the time.

The family never owned property (as far as I could tell) and by the 1881 census, the family was living in Granville Ferry, a short ferry ride from Annapolis Royal. Clara was 10, with older brother Frederick (11), younger brothers Minard (8) and Bud (2) and sister Nancy (4). Clara and her brothers attended school and Clara always reported that she could read and write on all census reports.

Charlotte Perkins was born in 1878 in Annapolis Royal, making her eight years younger than Clara,

21

and doubtless had nothing to do with Clara and her family in her early years. Charlotte's family owned the leading accommodations in Annapolis: first the Queen Hotel across from Fort Anne and then the Hillsdale House on upper St. George Street. They were formidable members of the Church of England and prominent fixtures of Victorian Annapolis Royal, so Charlotte's circle of activity and acquaintance would be distant from Clara's.

Charlotte was a great promoter of the history of her town, publishing, presenting and promoting our history from the 1920s through to the 1960s. Charlotte was always exceedingly fastidious in recounting the illustrious history of Annapolis Royal and her including Clara's story is most curious. One would have expected that this very proper guardian of the past and future of Annapolis Royal might have ignored Clara Sabean and Clara Beckwith, as her performing in water was suspect in proper Victorian times. But then Charlotte Perkins would have paid more attention to Mrs. Stanley McInnis (widow of a Manitoba legislator and dentist) when Clara came back to Annapolis Royal to open a hotel in 1909.

Charlotte's stories and 'romancing' have inspired much of the heritage preservation and interpretation of Annapolis Royal over the years. However, George and most others active in our venerable historical societies tend to dismiss her. Charlotte was not considered a 'proper historian', despite the success of her book. *The Romance of Old Annapolis Royal* has been continuously available for almost one hundred years. It was reprinted in 1934, 1952, 1978, 1985, 1988, and 2013, with the most recent edition expressing discomfort with Charlotte's "tenacious stereotypes".

Charlotte's description of Clara's early life (see page 171) is vivid, and maybe she did remember the young, enterprising Clara coming to the Queen Hotel, the Perkins family establishment on St. George Street in the heart of old Annapolis Royal. Charlotte would have been an impressionable eight years of age when Clara came by in a "tattered dress" and "bare feet" offering her marsh greens or begging at the age of 16.

George pronounced both the "tattered dress" and the house on Academy Square evidence of Charlotte's unreliability. The "tattered dress" he spotted as a Dickens cliché. Absolutely, Charlotte would have been reading Charles Dickens (and even seeking to emulate him), but she was also fastidious to a fault in her language, which was why she prefaced the "tattered dress" with "most likely".

George's research of the deeds of Annapolis Royal confirmed that the Sabeans had never owned a house in Annapolis Royal. They always rented, which they certainly could have done on Ritchie Street, behind the Grange, the Ritchie family mansion. Also, Clara travelling on the regular ferry (a steam ferry, the 'Joe Edwards', from 1881) between the Granville and Annapolis shores would have been the obvious way for Clara to get to Annapolis with its hotels and commerce in the 1880s.

Annapolis Royal had been connected to the world by railway in 1869, the year before Clara was born. George considered Clara's formative years, Annapolis' 'golden age'. It was the western terminus for the Windsor and Annapolis Railway, bringing visitors, goods and a building boom to Annapolis Royal. The steamers 'Empress', 'Evangeline' and 'Hunter' offered regular connections to New England. Weekly newspapers were begun and travelling entertainments came to 'Fullerton's' and the 'Academy of Music'.

A 12-year old Clara certainly would have taken in the Dominion Day Grand Gala at the Old Garrison Grounds, in 1882 with music furnished by a band from Windsor, Nova Scotia—which arrived on a special excursion train. One wonders which of the "games, swings, Aunt Sally, archery, croquet, and lawn tennis" Clara might have tried out.

Pursuing Clara

That same year Clara would have been watching the Annapolis Rink under construction and might well have roller-skated there, if she could afford the five-cent entry fee. Clara undoubtedly would have watched the roller-skating race for boys under 15 a couple of years later. Perhaps that gave her a sense of, and taste for, public competition, which was exploding in New England in the 1880s and 1890s.

Swimming at high tide in the Annapolis Basin would have been accessible to everyone—at least, anyone brave enough to negotiate the tides and temperatures. The world's highest tides off the Bay of Fundy certainly make swimming here cold and hazardous, but a small beach had formed in the lee of the Queen's Wharf. Braver locals and youngsters swam here and off 'Big Rock' in the French Basin.

Swimming was unconventional and largely unacceptable for respectable society in the 19th century. Water carried disease, pollution and human waste, certainly everywhere in the industrial world. Clothing of the time was made of natural fibres that held water, and was designed to enhance or camouflage the human body—making swimming difficult, if not impossible. Certainly any wet fabric clinging to and exposing the human body was scandalous. Swimming was dangerous, unhealthy and unsightly! Most people couldn't swim and 19th century newspapers regularly reported drownings.

Ironically, and particularly for those living on the sea or earning their living on water, swimming remained uncommon well into the 20th century. George succeeded in never swimming after suffering full-immersion baptism in the Annapolis Basin at Lower Granville late one November. He considered that sufficient for a lifetime, and was happy to avoid swimming thereafter.

Notable eccentrics promoted swimming. Leonardo da Vinci sketched life belts, and the first book on *The Art of Swimming* was published in Latin in 1587. In 1603 the Emperor of Japan declared that schoolchildren should learn to swim and Benjamin Franklin in the 18th century invented swimming fins among his many accomplishments.

Of course, kids always found swimming holes or beaches somewhere away from adult eyes and sensibilities. Annapolis had its tides to flush out whatever was being jettisoned off the Acadia Pier, and was small enough and far enough away from centres of conformity to evolve its own sense of propriety.

Annapolis also had W. W. 'Bert' Clarke, and Charlotte Perkins suggests (p. 169) that Clara and Bert Clarke were definitely known to each other.

Pursuing Clara

Bert Clarke, Clara's mentor in the water, was well-known in town. He was notorious for his passion for swimming and much else. George had a vivid memory of Uncle Bert in his 70s walking past the Crowe house on School Street in Annapolis Royal to swim at 'Big Rock' when the weather was not acceptable for anyone else. Bert Clarke was always promoting swimming, advancing the prestige of Annapolis Royal as a place for salt water swimming, and was urging town council to build bath houses at the King's Wharf off Fort Anne, according to the *Annapolis Spectator*[2].

Clarke was also somewhat of an idiosyncratic merchant in town, prompting the *Spectator* to comment in 1901:

> WW Clarke carries an assortment of groceries and fancy goods, as well as all the Ralston productions, and if, and when, he gets through selling you goods, you care to stay a while longer he can tell you lots of things about the Bible.

Clarke's store may have offered Annapolis Royal's first 'health food' options, and his garage, built after the 1921 fire, still survives at the northwest corner of Victoria and St. Anthony. One of George's friends remembers taking his bicycle there to be fixed and another actually has a letter in which Clark complained to his father of the mischief the young lads of town were inflicting on him.

Clarke died in 1950, but we do have people around who still remember those days. I continued to ask anyone of a certain age about Bert Clarke, and one local recalled Clarke's 'eye for the ladies of town'.

More than one recalled Clarke's nude sun-bathing down at the old King's Wharf, scaring the kids who were going down to swim at high tide. Maybe Bert Clarke had more to do with Clara than simply teaching her to swim? He would have been 21 to her 15 in 1885, making for a potential attraction, whether mutual or unreciprocated.

I wondered who else Clara might be hanging out with when growing up, and George found me an important lead. He has inexhaustible patience and memory for headstones (as do many genealogists) and spotted Harriet Hardwicke of Annapolis Royal as Bert Clarke's first wife.

Harriet Hardwicke was born in 1869, a year before Clara, and thus was most surely part of his swimming adventures in the Annapolis Basin. Harriet's younger sister Caroline would surely have tagged along, and Caroline became Clara's business partner many years later. Obviously they would have known each other well when growing up.

Clara's family did not show up in the *Spectator* during those years- so I could make no other speculation about Clara's friends.

I kept asking about the Wade and Sabean families, and George offered that the Wades (Clara's mother's family) were often foolish enough to swim in the Annapolis Basin and, indeed, to show off no matter what they were up to. George had a relative, Charlotte Wade, who told stories of floating through the underpinnings of the King's Wharf at high tide, and was of the right age to have heard stories of 'Aunt' Clara. Charlotte Wade was in the local nursing home when George put my questions to her, and she could only offer a bemused wordless smile in response to our queries.

I had spotted Charlotte's brother, Kemure Wade, as joining the 1935 Bert Clarke campaign to build bath houses at Fort Anne and would ask any 'Wade' I knew about their proclivity for swimming. Similarly, I pursued any Sabean/Sabin/Sabeans I might meet; but they tend to be a quiet, unassuming lot, not inclined to publicity. Charlotte Perkins telling of Clara's story did finally appear in one of their web-sites, but no one ever came forward with any memories, or the fabled scrapbook that maybe is out there somewhere. My car mechanic, Andrew Sabean, did ask his 90-year-old father about Clara, but he couldn't tell us anything.

I became something of a nuisance by asking for recollections from anyone whose lifespan would have overlapped with Clara's, and eventually learned to stop pestering anybody with a Sabean or a Wade connection.

Clara and her family emigrated to New England in the mid-1880s, though immigration records confirming Clara's arrival or departure have proven infuriatingly elusive. Records do confirm that Clara's mother, Jane Sabean, immigrated to the United States in 1886 with three children, whose names are not given. Perhaps Clara and/or her father had emigrated earlier or separately; or one of the children had died.

In later census reports Clara always offers 1887 as the year of her arrival in the United States, which agrees with Charlotte Perkins considering her 17 when she was travelling on the steamer 'Hunter' as it made one of its regular runs from Annapolis Royal to Boston.

I also came to believe that Clara's *In the Swim* inadvertently tells us how Clara began her transition to Clara Beckwith on her voyage to America. Her 1893 'autobiography' offers a vivid account of Clara saving a child where her "skill and physical powers proved masters of the trying situation and sustained the child above water fully twenty minutes before assistance could be rendered." (p. 125) Newspaper accounts much later confirm the child as a precocious sixteen-year-old son of a prominent family from Lynn, Massachusetts, travelling home via Nova Scotia from visiting England.

I was cautious about linking Charlotte's 1924 account of Clara leaving home and Clara's 'autobiography' in 1893, and George remains skeptical to this day. But then a Google search (with one of those serendipities that may be one of online searching's virtues) gave me confirmation of Clara's story. Indeed, this "drowning boy" eventually led to another male interest for Clara, but it is all too improbable until we understand Clara becoming Clara Beckwith, then Mrs. Stanley McInnis and eventually Mrs. Clement Miller.

Certainly we all agreed that Clara saving a young boy by jumping off the upper deck of a moving steamer into the Bay of Fundy would have caught everyone's attention and would have been reported. I set to work to confirm this story, and first searched out Frank Taylor, as he was working on his book, *Ghosts of Fundy*, on all the drownings and accidents on the Bay of Fundy. Frank was a friend and local researcher, and very much wanted to help, but had no record of such an event. Similarly the Admiral Digby Museum in Digby and the Saint John Maritime Museum found no confirmation of this life-saving off the steamer 'Hunter'.

George was now starting to avoid me at meetings we might attend, and it did take me years to eventually understand why this story might never have been reported or documented.

I wouldn't want you, my reader, to accept these assertions based on the evidence I have presented so far. But do keep these possibilities in mind as we follow Clara becoming the "world's champion lady swimmer", the mourning widow of a Manitoba legislator, a hotelier back in Annapolis Royal, and much, much else.

3: Clara Beckwith

Before Clara Sabean became Clara Beckwith, Agnes Beckwith and her older brother, Willie, came to America to demonstrate and promote swimming. In June of 1883 Agnes swam 15 of the 20 miles from Sandy Hook, New Jersey to Rockaway Pier, New York before a storm forced her out of the water "against her will".

Agnes and Willie also travelled to Toronto in 1883, where they were celebrated by the recently-established local swimming club. Agnes was back in the United States in 1886, now appearing with P. T. Barnum at Madison Square Garden. By this time she had married William Taylor, a theatrical agent who became an integral part of the Beckwith community of performance.

Agnes Beckwith continued performing until 1910, always being billed as the "premier lady swimmer of the world", though she never returned to North America after 1886.

The Beckwiths were invented by Frederick Edward Beckwith in Lambeth, England in the 1860s and 1870s. He taught and promoted swimming, publishing *The Whole Art of Swimming* in 1857. Historian Dave Day considers Beckwith instrumental in "pushing back the barriers to female swimming", as he explains in *Swimming Communities in Victorian England*[3]. Professor of Sports History at Manchester University, Dave Day has become a great friend in my 'pursuing Clara' and graciously used my research in his own publications.

Dave Day further explains that "Professor" Beckwith was also a licensed victualler and publican, tobacconist, father of seven children, and sometimes before the courts for various complaints. In his innovative and entrepreneurial fashion he introduced his two-year-old daughter, Agnes to the world in 1865, "greatly surprising the audience by her swimming and floating, although quite a baby." Then, recruiting students together with his family, the Beckwiths displayed "Feats of Natation" for paying spectators, including racing, endurance swimming, undressing, smoking and eating sponge cakes underwater, and much else from the 1870s to the 1890s.

On August 25, 1875 Matthew Webb was the first to swim the English Channel. A week later, on the 1st of September, Agnes Beckwith swam six miles of the Thames, from London Bridge to Greenwich. Both are considered milestones in the history of swimming and were promoted everywhere in the English-speaking world.

The Beckwiths were indisputably the first family of swimming and Charlotte Perkins, Caroline Hardwick and Bert Clarke clearly had the curiosity to have read about their exploits in the British newspapers that would have made their way to Annapolis Royal. Clara always reported that she could read in all census reports and maybe she was reading about Agnes Beckwith as well?

Figure 2: Agnes Beckwith

In the United States, women were curiously behind their British counterparts in physical and sporting activities. Catherine Beecher, an American educator of the time and well-known for her forthright opinions, complained: "In this nation it is rare to see a married woman of thirty or forty, especially in the more wealthy classes, who retains the fullness of person and the freshness of complexion that mark good health. But in England almost all women are in full perfection of womanhood at that point of life."[4]

Things were beginning to change. Vassar College from 1865 and Wellesley College from 1874 required all its female students to take calisthenics and sports, reflecting a changing attitude towards physical activity for women. Kate and Eliza Bennett were hosting water parties in floating, enclosed structures called 'baths' in the Hudson River from 1877, and offered lectures and demonstrations on the benefits of swimming. But all was in private, and certainly not for public appreciation, or for competition.

George doubts that a 17-year-old Clara Sabean from Granville Ferry would have had the imagination and courage to invent herself as a 'Beckwith'. It is very likely that someone convinced, instructed and promoted; or induced and seduced; or indentured and profited from Clara becoming a Beckwith.

Clara offers in her 1893 'autobiography' her British credentials: "Having been authoritatively informed that I was born in Lambeth, England, October 26th, 1867, I have long since accepted that assurance with passive resignation." (p. 113)

This is a most curious, off-hand way to claim a British lineage and sounds to me like Clara repeating what a manager or promoter had been insisting. Clara's "Autobiography of a Professional Swimmer" is also very careful about the Beckwiths, and particularly respectful towards her older sister, Agnes. It artfully perpetuates the Beckwith connection in giving Clara's father the name of the Beckwith older brother, William. Then it uses the name of Charles (Agnes' husband and agent) for a younger brother. It never contradicts anything known about the Beckwiths and effectively appropriates their fame and success for Clara.

I was convinced that Charlotte Perkins was becoming inventive when she considered her barefoot Clara a Beckwith and was ready to abandon my 'pursuing' when I sent Professor Day Clara's 'autobiography'. He pronounced Clara as "definitely not a Beckwith" and encouraged me to search out Clara's story further. Indeed, I eventually sent him my research and he made use of it in his essay "From 1860's Lambeth to Niagara: Imitation and Innovation Amongst Female Natationists", which we include (with permission) in our appendices.

Admittedly, Clara's earliest swimming in America has proven most difficult to confirm. Clara offers in her 'autobiography': "Two long and anxious years elapsed before an opportunity for a swimming contest was offered. My challenge was then accepted by a Miss St. John. The conditions were to swim (against time) over a three and a half mile course from Little Orchard Island to Fort Independence and return. Miss St. John proved to be a clever, strong swimmer, but my greater muscular development and endurance enabled me easily to defeat her." (p. 119)

Fort Independence was on Castle Island, one of several islands in Boston Harbour, but I was never able to find a Miss St. John or a Little Orchard Island, delighting George over and over again. My feeble response was that maybe her mentor/promoter/manager had not been able to secure any press coverage. I still expect that some community museum in New England has such confirmation, but maybe has not been able to digitize and download its holdings to the internet.

Clara's next swimming accomplishment is also elusive. "To my surprise and disappointment Leavitt retired from the contest after the first day. He was a fair swimmer, but lacked rapidity of movement and the enduring powers so essential to all professionals." (p.121) I spent a lot of time, and was equally disheartened, not able to confirm Clara's six-day race swimming against Leavitt, champion swimmer of Lowell, Massachusetts.

But a John A. Leavitt was being cited as a competitive swimmer as early as 1889 and celebrated in 1926 by the Brookline Swimming Club at its 30th anniversary as one of its pioneers. George offered that Clara, or her 'biographer', could have simply invented such a claim, using the name of an established swimmer to lend credence to her accomplishments. I countered that Clara may well have swum against a Miss St. John and a John Leavitt, in the summer of 1888, but these may have been impromptu or novel affairs, never gaining any publicity. We really don't know, and agreed to disagree.

Then, to further confuse and confound my research, another Miss Beckwith does show up in Boston in November of 1888, an Annie Beckwith. The *Boston Herald* on the 6[th,] November, 1888 describes

Pursuing Clara

Annie Beckwith as a first cousin of Agnes Beckwith, arriving to challenge anyone in the water.

Could this be Clara's first publicized appearance as swimmer? Certainly Annie's age and physique are close enough to Clara's in her 'autobiography'. Her blonde hair could be the blonde that Charlotte Perkins remembers and the 'dirty blond' that George assumes for her. Also, Annie Beckwith only ever appeared at the 'Boston Grand Dime Museum' where Clara Beckwith emerges under contract to George Lothrop two months later.

A six-day floating contest was organized at the 'Grand Dime' for Annie Beckwith, with Miss Rose Adams representing the "American colours", offering a $1,000 purse for whoever stays in the water the longest. The *Boston Herald* was a great supporter of this 'contest' and another one later in November.

Newspaper reports are effusive, though also unclear as to who wins these contests. (It probably didn't matter.) Then all the internet searching I could do, and all the Libbys I prevailed upon, never found another appearance for Annie Beckwith, certainly suggesting that Annie Beckwith was a short-lived invention. George remains convinced that Annie was an early incarnation of Clara, and she could well have been.

After the Christmas season of 1888-9, Clara is introduced to the world in the *Boston Globe* by the manager of the 'Boston Grand Museum', George Lothrop, who had recently taken over the 2600-seat venue with a heated swimming pool:

> *Miss Clara Beckwith will give exhibitions in the Natatorium of the Grand Museum, corner Washington and Dover Streets, for one week, commencing tomorrow at noon. Miss Clara Beckwith is the handsomest lady in America. She is the champion natator of the world. The management are ready to match her for a one- or six-day swim for one to five thousand dollars. Miss Clara Beckwith did accomplish last week, at this place, a feat that has never been attempted by any lady.*[5]

Clara's first competitor is Annie Fern, and maybe George Lothrop appreciated that he had a superior swimmer in Clara, more deserving of the Beckwith name, and 'retired' Annie Beckwith. Notice of Lothrop's 'ownership' of Clara Beckwith, once Clara's accomplishments had been demonstrated, appeared six months later:

> *Notice to the public: I have signed a contract not to exhibit at any place other than the Grand Museum and Natatorium, corner Washington and Dover Street. I am under five year's engagement to Manager Lothrop. Clara Beckwith.*[6]

From now, the newspapers regularly and faithfully reported Clara's success, with her besting Annie Fern, Maggie Dyas, Amy/Cora Rogers, May Morrison,

Pursuing Clara

Mary Sonson "the pretty Swede", Berthe Goodwin, Minnie/Katie Anderson, Rose Webb, Mamie Dassitt, a Miss Jordan, and other variations on these names. Newspaper coverage is inconsistent with every other name except Clara's. They always get Clara's name right!

And coverage of Clara's success was no longer limited to the *Boston Globe* and the *Boston Herald,* but included the *New York Times* and *New York Clipper*, the *Milwaukee Daily Journal*, the *Argos Reflector*, the *Buffalo Courier*, the *Rochester Tribune* and many others. Clara never again suffered from a lack of promotion or a lack of press coverage, and I have some 1,000 references by now for Clara competing and performing from 1889 to 1896. Indeed, do check out my timeline, beginning on page 201, as many more of Clara's accomplishments are chronicled there.

Even when her competitors combined their efforts, Clara invariably won, as the *Buffalo Courier* reported on the 7th of February, 1889:

> *A six-day female swimming match for the championship of America between Miss Clara Beckwith and a combination of ladies including Miss Fern, Miss Rogers, and Miss Dyas came to a close in Boston on Saturday night. Miss Beckwith won with a score of 35 miles, 39 laps against 28 miles, 21 laps scored by the combination, which Miss Dyas represented for the last 4 days of the race.*

Clara was so dominant in her swimming that the 'Grand Museum' had to invent new reasons for patrons to come and see her. Clara and her swimming colleagues did much more than just swim, just as the Beckwiths were doing in England and in Europe. They did somersaults, head walking, twisting, doubling, folding, diving, floating, dramatic tableaux, drowning and rescuing the drowning and some "fifty other difficult aquatic feats".

Each of the ladies had their own specialty. Cora Rogers apparently had lived in water for a record 106 days. Everything clearly was being invented, and often sounding like what we might now call water ballet or synchronized swimming.

Admittedly, Clara's accomplishments sound more than slightly bizarre or preposterous to our ears, but they seem perfectly restrained and admirable compared to the tickling contest attracting considerable revenue and making a sensation on YouTube as I write this.

The summer of 1889 was obviously a high point in inventing swimming for public viewing in Boston, and for July 4th another Beckwith made her appearance. Cora McFarland was born in 1869 in Maine and arrived in Boston as Cora Beckwith in the summer of 1889, promising demonstrations at Crescent Beach at Ocean Pier.

Clearly, many were noticing the success of the Beckwith name and the *Boston Globe* on the 3rd of July, 1889 announced:

> *ENGAGEMENT EXTRAORDINARY ON JULY 4TH – Cora Beckwith (the original), the world famous swimmer – Miss Beckwith must not be confused with any imitators who have used the name. She is the only original Miss Beckwith.... Among the various feats performed by Miss Beckwith are the straight dive, 90 somersaults under water, the tugboat, water waltz, hand walking, double floating, feet to feet, lifesaving, double somersault, and double back somersault.*

The management of the 'Grand Museum' was not amused, and published the following notice the next day. They clearly considered the Beckwith name their exclusive property:

> *NOTICE - Miss Clara Beckwith, champion lady swimmer of the world, is not in Boston, and will not appear at any swimming exhibition in America or England until she commences her fall engagement early in August at the Grand Natatorium, at the corner of Dover and Washington Streets under the management of G. E. Lothrop. Anyone using the name Beckwith as a swimmer to appear at any summer resort are doing so to deceive the public. Clara will be spending the summer at a cottage at Ocean Grove, New Jersey, with her mother and sister. She will not appear in public till the opening of*

> *the Grand Museum and Natatorium early in August."*[7]

Cora was not dismayed and appeared with John Leavitt at Crescent Beach on Coney Island and then at a mammoth tank "just completed at great cost and located in the museum annex of Pilling's World Museum in Boston."[8]

Clara, or her management, were determined to regain the upper hand in this battle for the Beckwith name and announced:

> *BECKWITH WILL SWIM ANY LADY - To the editor: From recent announcements that I have read in the Boston papers, I feel called upon in justice to the public and myself to state that I have not appeared in public since June 17th and will not appear again until late August. I again repeat my challenge to swim against any lady in the world for $500 or $1000 a side – Clara Beckwith, champion lady swimmer of the world.*[9]

'Pilling's World Museum' responded with an order to a Boston photographer for 100,000 photos of Cora Beckwith for free distribution.[10] Cora's photograph is difficult to find, given that newspapers were not yet publishing photographs, but Cora always had effusive publicity.

Clara was never photographed as performer, as Cora and many of her aquatic colleagues were.

George did not want to accept that a photo album, scrapbook, or even random photos do not survive somewhere, and he is hopefully still scouring eBay and yard sales for them. I contend that Clara never being photographed could add a reason to come and see her in person.

Nonetheless, more images of Clara than any of her contemporary swimmers actually appear in newspapers. She is always in her 'somber leotard', sketched in ink.

Wikipedia tells us that the leotard was first heard of in 1886, making Clara and her fellow natators' regulation leotards in the spring of 1889 an innovation, as well as more effective competitive attire. Historians of fashion or feminism insist that such clothing was scandalous until the 20th century and usually attribute the use of the leotard for swimming to Annette Kellerman in 1905. I spent countless hours looking for a hint of such scandal prompted by Clara, inviting Libby anywhere to find a record of Clara being disgraced.

Admittedly, a Boston alderman did protest a lithographed poster of Clara in front of the 'Grand Museum' in 1892. His protest never became a public issue but the trade press for the printing industry acknowledged: "In the poster picture she wears dark tights and has her neck and arms bare. The Museum manager regards it as a work of art and will frame a copy and show it in his Museum."[11] I always assumed that this would have been the sketch of Clara that adorns our cover, but this only made its appearance a year later when her 'autobiography' was published. You can be certain that I have followed up with all Boston museums, asking about this poster. I expect that it survives in some back room somewhere.

The 'Boston Grand Museum' was apparently closed for renovations early that summer of 1889 but by August were promising Clara's return: "RETURN OF LADY CHAMPION SWIMMER - Clara Beckwith, after an absence in New York of 10 weeks - Monster New Bath, 100 feet long, containing 100,000 gallons of water."[12]

Cora Beckwith was not going away, and was used by the 'Boston Grand Museum'. On the 11th of September, 1889 the *Boston Herald* reported:

> *THE RIVAL SWIMMERS - Miss Clara Beckwith, the swimmer, is satisfied that Miss Cora Beckwith has concluded to pay no attention to her recent challenge for a six-days swimming match. Miss Clara now offers her rival for the title of champion woman swimmer another chance to prove her superiority. She will swim Miss Cora Beckwith a six-day race and will let the latter name the hours for swimming, and she is now willing to place $2,000 against Cora's $1,000 that she will win the race. Furthermore Miss Clara will give her opponent five hours start but reserves the right to name the time and place of holding the match. A*

> *cheque for $500 has been left with the <u>Herald</u> in good faith.*

Cora and Clara never swam together. Indeed, how much swimming Cora ever did is unclear, but she successfully talked swimming for the rest of her life. Charles Ernest, the blackface minstrel performer, was her first manager, and was clearly adept at her promotions.

Cora and Clara apparently never crossed paths again, almost as if they were avoiding each other. Cora eventually married Jake Rosenthal, who was also her manager, and over the years she appeared in Chicago, San Francisco, the Toronto Industrial Exhibition, Buffalo, Kansas City and many points in between.

Cora's claims were always more extravagant than Clara's, or anyone else's. She regularly promised to swim Niagara Falls where Captain Mathew Webb had infamously drowned in 1883. The number of people Cora saved from drowning grew in virtually every newspaper account and a 6th of April, 1895 announcement in the *San Francisco Call* is typical:

> *Probably the greatest attraction ever visiting the coast is Miss Cora Beckwith, the champion swimmer of the world. Wherever she has appeared society has lionized her, and possibly would have spoiled her but for the brave little lady's level head. During her natatorial career she has saved forty-nine persons from a wa-*

> tery grave, and in consequence she holds medals from three nations. She would never accept pecuniary rewards. In company with the late Captain Webb (who lost his life in the attempt to swim the rapids of Niagara) she started from Dover, England and swam the English Channel, landing at Calais, France, a distance of twenty-one miles, and as every navigator knows, as ugly a stretch of water as can be found. She will, unless friends dissuade her, attempt to swim the rapids of Niagara the 2nd of next June.

Eventually Cora led a troupe of acts, and was still touring when she died at the age of 48 of pneumonia in 1924. Every notice of Cora references her Beckwith family origins; though only in 1897, once Clara 'retires', does Cora elaborate on her Lambeth swimming experience, almost as if she is quoting from Clara Beckwith's *In the Swim*.

By the fall of 1889 Clara's prowess at swimming may have been discouraging other competitors, and a purse was offered for anyone, male or female, to take her on.

My timeline was necessary to organize all the challenges and accomplishments of Clara. George was not impressed and insisted that Clara Beckwith was nothing more than an elaborate promotional stunt to attract new audiences for the Boston Grand Museum. George also offered that these six-day races, with many different competitors, would have provided wonderful ongoing opportunities for gambling. He is undoubtedly right, but the prospect of gambling surely does not diminish the risk-taking and innovation in the water being witnessed in Boston.

Absolutely many of the 'races' sound more like performances than sports, though the distinction between sports and performance may be as vague in the 1890s as it is today. My work with the past has taught me to be wary of 'presentism', where we assume we are more enlightened and rational than earlier times. So I am prepared to consider Clara seriously as 'Modern Mermaid' just as I appreciated 'King' James versus 'Cunning' Curry in the National Basketball Association championships in the spring of 2016. The National Basketball Association front office was clearly delighted with the unprecedented Cleveland win after going down three games to one, and certainly earned everyone (including online gambling sites) more substantial revenues with the series going to seven games. But all of that didn't diminish the accomplishment of the Cleveland Cavaliers and Lebron James!

Returning to Clara's story, a more serious contender, Valeksa Nelson of Germany, took up Clara's challenge in September, 1889:

> *Valeska Nelson puts up $500 for race with Clara Beckwith: Valeska Nelson, the Champion swimmer of Germany, wants to swim Clara Beckwith, Champion swimmer of America. Nel-*

> son called the Globe office yesterday and stated that she would like to meet Beckwith in such a race, and expressed herself as confident of winning. "I can put up $1,000 she said,... Furthermore I agree to swim her in the natatorium where she has been doing all of her swimming.[13]

Nelson reserved the right to appoint her referee and to limit how many hours a day they would be swimming in a six-day match billed as "Germany vs the World". Clara pulled ahead each day and this may be where she set the record that she claimed in her 'autobiography': "My record was 74 ½ miles. I could have added five miles to my score, but the conditions of the race did not justify the extra exertion." (p.121)

Clara needed a rest after the summer of 1889, and one press notice has her visiting Europe though she must have been doing so privately as no press notices of her ever appeared. Then in the spring of 1890 a novel attraction was offered at the 'Howard Atheneum' combining drama and swimming, in a play called *A Dark Secret*. This attraction somehow involved a "very handsome" Henley regatta boat race with the highlight being:

> a swimming race for $250 between Miss Clara Beckwith and Miss Katie Anderson. The ladies are to swim one quarter of a mile each evening of the week, and the one winning the most events Saturday is to be named the final win-

> ner. Miss Beckwith won the event last evening in 6 minutes 22 seconds, gaining one lap on her opponent. This race was much enjoyed in the upper part of the house, but the swimmers were invisible from the orchestra floor.[14]

When the renovated 'Grand Museum' was reopened by the end of July, 1890, Clara led her "bevy of female coadjutors blindfolded in the water" offering a "doughnut chase" and much else. Now George was becoming quite disgusted with me and I have left much of the enthusiasm of the Boston newspapers for the timeline.

But a notice that the 'Harvards' had recruited Clara to captain their team caught my attention. Libby, at Harvard University Library, sent me the newspaper report of what these ladies were up to:

> Yale vs Harvard, as exemplified by the lady swimmers at the Grand Museum, corner of Washington and Dover streets, yesterday proved most attractive. The Harvards were captained by Miss Clara Beckwith, champion swimmer of the world, and the Yales by Miss Mary Anderson, champion all-round athlete. The bouts were of an exciting nature, and it was evident to members of the audience that both teams were in earnest in their effort to conquer. The bounding ball was kept in constant motion and when the inflated globe was

> *hurled over the goal by either side the applause was hearty and deserved.*[15]

The few female students at Harvard in the 1890s were absolutely not doing anything so vigorous and sporting as this, and Clara did not receive an athletic scholarship to bolster their ranks. Rather, George Lothrop at the 'Grand Museum' was inventing another 'attraction' for prospective audiences.

Obviously, it was a precursor to water polo these ladies were playing at, though whether as a sport or performance is difficult now to say. Libby, in charge of the Kinesiology collection at Acadia University, found for me a reference to the invention of water polo a decade later, so Clara and her colleagues may well have a claim to inventing the sport.

Clara took another break in the winter of 1890-91, or maybe the 'Boston Grand Museum' closed its 'natatorium'. Then, in the summer of 1891, Clara began offering outdoor swimming exhibitions. In November she made her first appearance in New York City at 'Proctor's Theatre and Pleasure Palace' (a vaudeville standard).

Press notices for Clara were now becoming less effusive, and George contends that audiences were getting tired of Clara. Clara completely disappeared from public notice for twelve months, from November 1891 to November 1892, and I was becoming concerned for her.

Clara performed again at the 'Grand Museum' in Boston in November of 1892 with the *Boston Herald* almost sounding as if they are saying goodbye to "Miss Clara Beckwith, who has made so many friends at this house".

Clara was now performing in a tank on stage and introduced a new element:

> *SPLASH, TERROR, DEATH - A splash means that daintily attired little affair will drop itself into the water. Terror means that the act will make you feel very uncomfortable. It is a human nature feeling. It comes over you because you think the poor creature is drowning. Death, well death means when you quit trouble. You will think that the gingerly trimmed little lady is drowned. You will think that her narrow little brain has gone to the bottom of the tar swabbed tank, or gone to her God, but it don't. She will blossom out as BECKWITH, the champion, the beautiful, the angelic at the Grand Museum.[16]*

Indeed, Clara explains her drowning in her 'autobiography': do check out her own words, starting on page 123.

Clara next brings her tank performances to the 'Monumental Theatre Annex Auditorium' in Baltimore in December of 1892, and thereafter considers Baltimore her home in America.

Clara clearly has someone promoting her more widely than ever before and the French wax-worker and sculptor working in Baltimore, Nero de Berselli, announced in late December of 1892 that Clara was the most "perfectly formed body" in the world, and that she would become his model for his statue "The Diving Girl".

Indeed, George, and anybody hearing that I am working on Clara Beckwith, send me "MEASUREMENTS OF A SWIMMING GIRL" over and over again:

> *Miss Beckwith's measurements are perfect and besides she has development of muscle with no superfluous flesh. Her head in length measures 9 ½ inches, so does her foot; her chest measures 39 inches; and she can easily expand it three inches more; her hip measures forty inches, upper arm 12 ½ inches and her lower arm 10 ½ inches. The measurements of the neck should be equal to that of the calf, but my model's neck is 13 ½ inches whereas the measurement of the calf is 14 inches. My work will not be original because it will be a reproduction of the well-known picture of the diving girl with her hands raised above the head and just about to make the leap. My model will, however, will allow me to add new grace and beauty to the subject.*

This report was reprinted in newspapers around the world with the *Colorado Transcript* cheekily asking "Who Measured Her?" George, of course, offered a 'cheekier' observation that she surely would have sculpted in the nude. I encouraged him, thinking that this possibility might prompt him to find the statue.

Indeed, I made dozens of inquiries to museums asking for the whereabouts of this statue, to no avail. The World Wide Web proclaims "The Diving Girl" an invention of Jantzen swimwear in 1916, so again Clara from Granville Ferry was way ahead of her time.

George, of course, reminded me that an announcement does not make for a statue actually existing, and I triumphantly produced a notice of its appearance in February, 1893 at the 'Howard Auditorium', and then at Kernan's Lyceum Theatre in Washington DC at the end of May, 1893. Then I remembered Charlotte Perkins telling us that Clara's swimming mentor back in Annapolis, Bert Clarke, had recognized Clara from her statue when going into a Washington art gallery. (p. 174)

I had been ignoring Charlotte on this strange assertion, but now renewed my efforts to locate this statue.

Clara's statue makes another 'appearance' a year later in a "theatrical chat" column in the *Washington Post*: "Another man declared that the living picture of the diver was nothing more or less than the plaster cast of Clara Beckwith, the swimmer who was at Kernan's last summer."[17]

The statue is never heard of again, and maybe survives in some private collection. Indeed, I am wondering how long Nero de Berselli stayed in America, or continued sculpting, as no Libby anywhere could find any traces of him.

Clara's 'autobiography', *In the Swim*, came out early in 1893, also from Baltimore. You can read the complete text in our appendix. None of the other swimmers of this era can boast of anything similar, not even Agnes Beckwith, and I will always be wondering about the authorship of *In the Swim*. Admittedly the 'autobiography' sounds florid and contrived to our 21st century ears, but Charlotte Perkins would have liked it, and surely would have referenced if she had ever seen it.

George would not let me claim it for Clara, and I had to admit that it was highly unlikely that Clara had authored this herself. I challenged, invited and begged my academic friends to compare *In the Swim* with other late 19th century texts. Maybe the automated, digital plagiarism-checking tools used to monitor students' essays could be applied historically, and we could find something else written by the same author?

In the Swim obviously uses as its model *The Whole Art of Swimming*, published almost 40 years earlier. Both were of a similar scope and direction, urging readers to take up swimming, and both began with Benjamin Franklin's advice on swimming. But the wording of the text is not the same and *The Whole Art of Swimming* does not include the sort of biographical or personal details that *In the Swim* offers. The 1857 volume stresses the practical advantages of learning to swim, whereas *In the Swim* in

1893 offered more technical direction and promoted the holistic value of swimming. Clara's 'autobiography' obviously used the earlier book as its inspiration, but never plagiarized or repeated anything from it.

Clara's actual father being artfully disguised, confirmation of many of Clara's competitors and colleagues, and then the eventual confirmation of her 1886/87 rescue of the "youngste*r*" from drowning in the Bay of Fundy (see more in chapter 7) illustrated and recounted in *In the Swim*, all gave me growing confidence in the reliability of the 'Autobiography of Miss Clara Beckwith'. But do read it for yourself, as it undoubtedly carries further clues as to Clara's collaborator, promoter, or friend who authored it.

Curiously, the dozens of articles that make use of *In the Swim* never reference it directly, though one easily recognizes phrases and even complete sentences from it. Similarly, one of the 12 sketches of Clara, demonstrating various swimming strokes, in her tank "walking on her hands, or taking a header" frequently appear in newspaper coverage thereafter.

At Kernan's Lyceum Theatre in Washington, through the month of June of 1893, Clara offered daily exhibitions at 3, 5, 9, 10, & 11 in their Summer Garden, where a tank 60 feet long was eventually erected for her:

> *Miss Clara Beckwith, champion lady swimmer of the world gives exhibitions in a large tank in*

> the theatre. A group of lights is placed behind the tank so that every movement in the water may be seen by the audience. The exhibition of Miss Beckwith is remarkable and her imitation of how a person drowns is thrillingly interesting. Miss Beckwith eats, sleeps, drinks and plays cards under the water and has a record of holding her breath two minutes and forty-five seconds.[18]

Kernan's also introduced a tournament of female pedestrianism in June of 1893, offering Clara's exhibition in the intervals while the women 'race-walkers' were taking a break.

Kernan's was charging a princely sum of 24 cents admission for Clara's performances, and the *Washington Evening Star* became a great fan, reporting that:

> Manager Kernan will regret her departure, which other engagements necessitate. Miss Clara Beckwith will positively make her last appearance at Kernan's Lyceum Theatre in Washington next week. It is doubtful whether at any time in the history of this house a star has evoked more admiration than Miss Beckwith. Young, beautiful and graceful, with all the dexterity and daring of a fabulous mermaid she presents an act that possesses that novelty which never wears off. Her extended performance of four weeks is a new experience

> to the patrons though in Baltimore under James R. Kernan's management she appeared for over six months. Other engagements interfering, however, Miss Beckwith cannot remain longer than next week. This should be born in mind as well as the hours of her appearance, 5, 9 & 10 pm.[19]

In July, Clara moved on to New York City, performing at 'Tony Pastor's' (Pastor is sometimes called the father of vaudeville).

> Clara Beckwith, the eighth wonder of the world can live, eat, walk, play, waltz, read, and act under water and is performing at Tony Pastor's Theatre – New York. She will be seen in a glass tank 4 feet by 14 feet, 8 feet deep. Her appearance will be decidedly seasonable and her audience will probably be inclined to envy her luxury of a constant cold water bath.[20]

Clara was very busy the summer of 1893, between Kernan's Lyceum Theatre in Washington and Tony Pastor's in New York City. Indeed, she alternated between these cities for the next few years, obviously moving her tank to wherever she was performing.

> Clara Beckwith, expert swimmer, was expecting to begin her performance at Proctor's

> *Pleasure Palace three weeks ago but is being compelled to rest because her tank was lost by the railway company and has been found at some out of the way place. She will be suing the railway company for her enforced idleness.*[21]

Clara *may* also have been retained for three weeks at Sommer Park and the Laurentian Bath in Montreal in September 1893, *maybe* floated for 40 days at the Casino in Chicago in October of 1894, and *perhaps* made an appearance at the Atlanta Exposition in November 1895. I certainly hoped that Clara had appeared at the Toronto Industrial Fair in August of 1895, but had many notices of her making regular appearances in Washington and Baltimore that same month!

I followed up on all of these notices and many more, but was not able to confirm them to my satisfaction. Clara's excellent promotions were causing some confusion between her and Cora from 1893 on. Indeed, at one point Cora's husband, Jake Rosenthal, is reported as promoting Clara. This I discounted as simply newspaper confusion and perhaps also explained Clara being referenced where Cora was repeatedly performing.

Similarly, Clara Beckwith was being credited as late as 1913 with the Agnes Beckwith swim in the Thames back in the 1870s. This was evidence of her enduring reputation. Notice of Clara in 1917 offering 'balloon ascensions" I would like to consider 'my' Clara coming out of retirement!

Clara did swim on behalf of the pension fund of the Pilots' Benevolent Association at the 5th Ave Theatre In New York City in June, 1895. Cora was usually the one demonstrating all the lives she had saved but publicity for this appearance clearly drew on Clara's 'autobiography' and featured her three life-saving stories:

> *Clara Beckwith will be demonstrating how to save people from drowning. This exhibition will be given in a huge glass tank, containing many hundreds of gallons of water that has been shipped from Boston and will be placed on stage of the Fifth Ave Theatre the evening before the performance. Miss Beckwith was among the first to offer the pilots her services and will travel a long distance to be present and offer her share of the entertainment.* (New York Herald)

George, early in my curiosity about Clara, one day left me the cryptic voice mail: "Clara Speaks!" He had found Clara Beckwith offering instructions on learning to swim in the November 1895 issue of *Good Health* magazine, published by Kellogg's of Battle Creek, Michigan (an early health food publication). It summarized her philosophy of swimming using identical phrasing from *In the Swim* and was presumably submitted by the same friend/promoter/manager who authored that book with Clara.

Here and elsewhere, Clara challenged American women to follow the example of their British cousins. Clara always had a holistic view of swimming. Repeatedly she spoke of her life "in the water as preserving her health in all seasons, as the highest type of physical culture, as inspiring self-confidence that seems to cling to us through life and a perfectly healthful condition of mind and body." (p. 131)

Indeed, Clara represented humility in her 'autobiography', claiming that she had no use for press notices:

> *I am grateful for the fact that my nature is not susceptible to flattery otherwise the success I have attained might have proved a question of serious doubt. Naturally, I am proud of the distinction of being recognized as the 'Champion Lady Swimmer of the World' but my pride exists alone in the truth that my honours have been acquired by perseverance, hard work, and a determination to win unquestionable success in my life's vocation.* (p. 117)

By the end of 1895 Clara's 'attraction' was apparently fading. She was sounding more like another vaudeville attraction who could be slotted in between elephants, a burlesque bullfight, sword-fighting acts and the like. And once, in August of 1895, the *New York Herald* acknowledged that Clara was ill and had to postpone her appearance.

Press notices of Clara fall off significantly in 1896; but then, somehow, Clara found herself at the Industrial Exhibition in Winnipeg and at the Brandon Fair in the summer of 1897. Her Manitoba visit begins a very new chapter for Clara, who never performed or competed again, though she retained the Beckwith name for decades.

Or maybe Clara never stopped performing, competing, innovating and imitating?

MRS. McINNIS
The Bereaved Wife of the Late Hon. Stanley W. McInnis.

Figure 3: Mrs. Stanley McInnis

4: Mrs. Stanley McInnis

Clara returned to Manitoba in November of 1897, either being courted or doing the courting of Stanley W. McInnis, a dentist in Brandon, Manitoba. She was now not the 'champion swimmer': social notes simply mentioned that a Clara Beckwith was staying at the Manitoba Hotel.

I submit that Stanley was smitten by Clara at one of her performances in New England, and maybe even facilitated her coming to Manitoba for her performances in the summer of 1897. Certainly Stanley McInnis was an organizer, and a mover and shaker in Brandon, with connections that could have facilitated Clara visiting Brandon that summer.

However, they connected, Stanley Wm McInnis and Clara May Beckwith were married on the 23rd of February, 1898 in Hamilton County, Ohio. The Probate Judge and Deputy Clerk witnessed the wedding, conducted by a clergyman of the Protestant Episcopal Church. Parents from both families are conspicuously absent from the marriage record—and why Ohio? I never could find any rationale, other than Ohio being in a line between New England and Brandon. Perhaps it combined a convenient halfway point with anonymity for Clara and Stanley.

Their marriage was not the noteworthy event in Brandon that George and I would have expected, given Stanley's local status. Indeed, it was never mentioned in local papers, implying that Clara's previous life in New England 'natatoriums' and illuminated tanks made her a dubious match for the successful dentist and aspiring public figure.

Still, one would expect that Stanley and Clara could hardly escape notice in Brandon in the first decade of the 20th century. He was President of the Manitoba Dental Association; founder of the Canadian Dental Association; organizer of the Brandon Fire Insurance Company and President of the Brandon Horticulture Society. Stanley McInnis was also involved in provincial politics; elected to the Manitoba Legislature in 1899, 1903 and 1907, and served as Provincial Secretary and Minister of Municipal Affairs for the province from 1907. In his spare time he was known as a fine baritone singer; a cartoonist; President of the Brandon Baseball team, the Brandon Gun Club, the Brandon Athletic Club and the Brandon Turf Club; and fund-raiser for the Provincial Sanatorium in Brandon.

According to the Ancestry web-site report for the Canadian census of 1901, Stanley and Clara were living in Brandon with two domestics. Clara was now listed as being born in England on October 26th, 1873 (the birth date from her 'autobiography'). And Stanley and Clara had a seven-year old son, William!

George immediately considered him Stanley's son, born before Clara and Stanley got together—at least until I reminded him that Stanley left William Tuckey nothing in his will, even though he provided for a godson. Then actually looking at the census record it is clear that the seven-year old was the child of one of their servants, Elizabeth Tuckey (who immigrated from Ireland in 1882).

In any case, a young boy would surely have been fascinated with Clara's performing/competing life (if she admitted to it) and I had to follow up with his story and potential descendants. He would have lots of questions for Clara and would have been the one to pore over Clara's scrapbook over and over again!

I challenged George to follow this youngster, but the best we could do was to find a William George Tuckey buried in the Edmonton Municipal Cemetery in 1914 at the age of 21, without an obituary.

Stanley and Clara lived at the corner of 6th and Victoria Streets, on one of those boulevards with a grassy strip, which would have been a fashionable address, and perhaps now one of Brandon's historic properties. George again came to the rescue, remembering an old friend, now active with the local heritage society. She sadly confirmed that Stanley and Clara's house had not survived. So I had no opportunity to visit Clara in Brandon.

Despite Stanley McInnis' prominence in Brandon and Manitoba affairs, Clara, as Mrs. Stanley McInnis, is strangely missing from the gossip columns in the local or Winnipeg newspapers. After diligent digital searching, Clara finally made an appearance (six years after they were married) as patroness of an 'At Home' for the bachelors of Brandon and pouring tea for the social event of the season as reported in the *Brandon Daily Sun* on the 23rd January, 1904: "An 'at home' given by Mrs. Cumberland Friday afternoon at her pretty new home in honour of and to say goodbye to Mrs. J. C Nicoll, who is leaving Brandon for New York....and Mrs. McInnis poured tea and coffee from four to five."

But Clara never became a regular on the Brandon social scene, with only a single further notice of her attending another 'at home' in the spring of 1904. These years might have been awkward or refreshing for Clara, a contrast to her very public life in the 1890s. Perhaps Clara and Stanley were trying to have children? Having two servants implies considerable entertaining, but the social notes of local newspapers never hint of this. Maybe this is a function of the incomplete scanning and digitizing of Manitoba newspapers, or my own limitations with digital searching? I had professional archival colleagues working in Manitoba, but never could stimulate a Libby or a genealogist to take my research further into Clara's life in Brandon.

Stanley McInnis owned an impressive range of properties, including a farm at the eastern limits of Brandon where Clara's favourite brown mare 'Maud' was kept. Stanley left 'Maud' to Clara in the settlement of his estate, but whether she ever actually rode horses I was not able to confirm.

Stanley McInnis died very suddenly from an attack of appendicitis, with Clara at his side, in November 1907. He put his affairs in order in his final days, making very specific arrangements for all of his properties and bequests. Stanley McInnis was now given great coverage and Clara's photograph was in the *Brandon Sun*.

George observed that Clara here looked remarkably similar to her promotional lithograph of 14 years earlier, though now looking appropriate to her station in life. The dimple in her chin and her short curly hair in both the *Brandon Sun* picture and her 1893 'autobiography' suddenly gave her 1893 lithograph more credibility than I had dared imagine. Thank you, George!

The *Manitoba Free Press* spoke of McInnis's "breadth of thought, independence of view and freedom from petty ideas" making him "an ornament to the legislature and a valued asset in the public life of Manitoba."[22]

The city of Brandon proclaimed November 7, 1907 a public holiday to allow citizens to attend the Stanley McInnis funeral at Saint Matthew's Anglican Church, with a procession from their residence. All provincial politicians attended, along with many notable citizens, as the *Brandon Daily Sun* duly noted: "Never before in Brandon has such an awe-inspiring sight been witnessed. The Wheat City paid tribute to the departed member in a manner that showed only too well the unspeakable admiration held for him by all."

A special train was organized to take the body to Winnipeg, where Stanley McInnis was buried at the Brookside Cemetery. In his honour the city of Brandon established Stanley Park, at the corner of Princess and 15th Streets, where today one can enjoy the water park; play tennis, basketball, or volleyball; lawn bowl or have picnics.

Stanley McInnis left to Clara their home with all of its contents, except for his library (left to his brother, Arthur P. McInnis). The Stanley McInnis estate included 37 separate properties and was estimated at $152,844.89. Small amounts were designated for a step-mother in California, a brother and a godson, with 70% reserved so that $1,000 could be paid annually to his "dear wife, Clara McInnis, for her lifetime", with the balance thereafter going to the Provincial Sanatorium.

Clara did receive payments from the McInnis estate for the rest of her life and the probate court records afford us some tantalizing, though sporadic, clues as to her whereabouts. The probate records yield few other hints of Clara though they document, at great length, the management of Stanley McInnis properties and estate funds over the years.

Clara had obviously not developed any affection or loyalties for Brandon and, with some detours, ended up back in Annapolis Royal. She apparently had fond memories from her childhood, just as Charlotte Perkins suggested.

5: C. M. McInnis

Clara had not forgotten about Nova Scotia in her 20 years as Clara Beckwith and as Mrs. Stanley McInnis, and had aspirations for herself and her old town, Annapolis Royal. Charlotte Perkins recounts that Clara "used to watch the grand Ritchie house grow and wish she could own it some day—a dream she never lost sight of. The Sabeans then lived in a small house on Academy Square." (p.175)

Clara would have been five, living a short walk from the imposing Ritchie residence being built on St. George Street in 1875. Ian Lawrence, a community historian who grew up in the Hillsdale House across St. George Street from the Ritchie mansion, writes:

> *In the Victorian style of the day, the Richie house featured everything on a grand scale; the ceilings were tall, the staircase large, the mouldings heavy. A balustrade fence, with gates at either end of the driveway, enclosed the property. Ritchie, already known to be of litigious nature, refused to take over the house, claiming it was not to his specifications. During the lawsuit that followed, the public roamed freely through the building.*[23]

Clara would thus have had a vivid memory of the old Ritchie home when it came up for sale and the Annapolis Spectator reported on the 13th of January, 1909: "Mrs. C. McInnis left Thursday on a trip to Montreal. Before leaving she gave orders to have the Ritchie mansion fitted up for occupancy. It is generally understood that she has purchased the property."

George's research into the deeds of Annapolis Royal confirms that Clara purchased the St. Andrew's School (as the Ritchie mansion was then known) and property for $3,000 on February 8th, 1909, and a few days later took out a mortgage with Caroline Hardwicke (spinster from Boston) for $2,000.

But who was Caroline Hardwicke? Caroline was born in Annapolis Royal in 1874, and George somehow remembered seeing a photo of 'Carrie' Hardwicke in an Annapolis Academy class photo in Ian Lawrence's book *Historic Annapolis Royal*, in which she is seated in the row above Charlotte Perkins. Annapolis Royal and Granville Ferry have always been small worlds, further supporting Charlotte Perkins, Caroline Hardwicke and Clara Sabean knowing each other when they were growing up.

Then, looking up Caroline's mother's obituary, George spotted a reference to Caroline teaching at Wellesley College, one of the earliest and most prominent educational institutions for women in the

United States. Of course, they have an archive, and Libby there found a file with an obituary for Caroline dying in 1919. This led back to Acadia Ladies' Seminary, where another Libby found her as "Carrie" taking classes from 1893 to 1897.

After Acadia, Caroline received diplomas in Culture, Teaching and Philosophy from the Curry School of Expression in Boston. She taught at Tudor Hall School in Indianapolis, Bridgewater State Normal School, Tuckerman School and eventually Wellesley College near Boston.

Caroline teaching Expression, Reading and Speaking at the auspicious Wellesley College intrigued me. I asked Libby at Wellesley College to find me something Caroline might have written and published, to no avail. I wanted to believe that Caroline had collaborated with Clara in the writing of *In the Swim*, but my timeline diminished that possibility. Caroline was only 19 and not yet at school at Acadia Ladies' Seminary in Nova Scotia, and therefore not likely having any regular contact with Clara, who had been in New England for at least five years by the time that the 'autobiography' was published in 1893.

My timeline also reminds us that Caroline only arrived in New England after Clara left for Brandon—but maybe they corresponded all these years, as lots of young women were doing. Or maybe Clara and

Caroline reconnected when the grieving Mrs. Stanley McInnis came back to New England in 1907/08.

Then George, with his interminable curiosity and memory for head-stones, spotted Caroline's older sister, Mrs. Harriette Clarke, as Bert Clarke's wife, who died in 1908. This would certainly be a reason for Caroline to reconnect with her family in her native Annapolis Royal. Also, George found Mrs. Harriette Clarke operating a millinery establishment in Annapolis Royal, and Caroline herself opening a millinery store in Wolfville, both precursors to Clara's and Caroline's entrepreneurial ambitions in Annapolis Royal.

George spotted Clarke being a widower in 1909, when Clara came back to Annapolis Royal, and wondered what they might have been up to together. This the *Annapolis Spectator* was not going to tell, and though George and his buddies had stories of Bert Clarke's eye for the ladies, none of them were old enough to remember Clara.

The Annapolis Royal Pickwick Club was at its height in the early 20th century, with Charlotte Perkins involved in all of its projects. The Pickwick Club was a women's group where members discussed and presented music, theatre and tableaux, and surely would have been most interested in Clara as 'Clara Beckwith'. Indeed, Charlotte Perkins was in-

Pursuing Clara

variably the photographer of the Pickwick Club activities, and thus could well have photographed Clara when Clara was opening the Ritchie home as a hotel, 'The Old Orchard House', in June of 1909.

I dragged George into one of our two local historical societies and insisted that we pore over every photograph of Charlotte's and of the Pickwick Club. He has an uncanny visual memory and would be able to spot Clara by comparison with her 1907 Brandon photograph, if she was ever photographed back in Annapolis. An undated photo of an Annapolis Royal Pickwick Club picnic looked particularly promising and we spotted much that delighted both of us—but no Clara!

George proposed other collections that we could look into. I invited him to find what he could find there, and returned to Charlotte, as I had come to have great faith in her.

Charlotte Perkins herself would have been 29 when Clara came back and undoubtedly watched with great interest a new hostelry being established in Annapolis Royal.

> *One day there was quite a flutter in town, for Clara was coming back to fulfill her dreams – to buy the Ritchie house. She brought a friend with her, also a lot of baggage. She called the*

> place, 'The Old Orchard House', from the old orchard to the south of it, and began to get ready for tourists. Business boomed in the old town, for she ordered all the best furnishings the merchants could provide – but with promissory payments. (p.176)

But who was the 'friend' Charlotte referenced here? If it was Caroline Hardwicke, why not name her, as Charlotte loved to insert as many names into her history as possible? The Hardwickes would have been a prominent family to reference (even if they were Methodists, not Anglicans like the Perkins family). Never finding confirmation that Caroline came back to Annapolis Royal that summer, I have no idea how active she may have been with Clara and the operation of 'The Old Orchard House'.

Again my timeline came to the rescue, as Clara married a Clement Miller on the 25th of November, 1908, a year after Stanley McInnis died and only six weeks before she purchased the Ritchie property. Another improbable re-invention of Clara that I would have to research, and another chapter in my 'pursuing Clara'. But if Clara was presenting herself in Annapolis Royal as Mrs. C. M. McInnis or simply as C. M. McInnis, then Charlotte Perkins would indeed have been discrete enough to refer to Clement Miller as a 'friend'.

George read and indexed every surviving issue of the *Annapolis Spectator* for the years in question both at the Annapolis Heritage Society and at the Public Archives of Nova Scotia. I gave him a ride to Halifax and he had inexhaustible patience for going through old newspapers. He found ads in the *Spectator* throughout July, 1909, advertising Clara's latest venture.

> *Old Orchard House, Annapolis Royal, NS*
> *Beautiful Grounds, Airy Rooms, Modern Equipment*
> *Fishing, Boating, Bathing and Tennis*
> *Good Service - C M McInnis*

Clara invited locals to inspect the facility and Charlotte Perkins sounds like she attended this reception. She would have followed the progress of the 'Old Orchard House' with great interest, given her view from the Hillsdale House, just across St. George Street, which her family then owned:

> *Her house in order, she gave a large reception one evening, and with her friend, graciously received her guests; a large French music box*

> *played, while refreshments were served in the dining room. How did the townspeople react? There were those who scoffed – 'wouldn't think of going', knowing her background. Some went for business reasons. Some out of curiosity, while other just to be neighborly, for hadn't she came to live amongst us?* (p.177)

But not all went well that summer of 1909 and Charlotte Perkins offers her 1924 version of Clara abandoning her project in her *Romance of Old Annapolis Royal*:

> *The tourist season was slim that summer, not what she had anticipated, and she had spent considerable money on the place. So, with her resources running low, she suddenly decided to decamp. One evening, she called the firm of Chas Dargie & Son, telling them they could have the furniture back as it was just as good as when she bought it. The next morning word quickly got around that she was leaving town with bills not paid! One of her creditors got out 'a capais' but not soon enough for Clara, for when the policeman arrived with it at the station she was already on the train, waving a calm and smiling good-bye. The merchants af-*

terwards recovered most of their goods. (p.177)

But then George, completely unexpectedly and to his own surprise, found another version of Clara becoming hotelier in Annapolis Royal. Will R. Bird, the Nova Scotian novelist and travel writer, wrote about a visit to Annapolis Royal in the 1950s in *These are the Maritimes*. Bird admitted to relying on Charlotte Perkins and tells Clara's story, albeit with intriguing variations:

> *Her kind friend and manager died suddenly and she placed her affairs in the hands of a lawyer and made a trip back to the scene of her childhood. The big house was empty and she decided she would make her name in the town. She bought the building, ordered all the dishes and furnishings needed, hired a staff, invited all the social elite to a grand opening night and engaged the local orchestra on the occasion. She had kept in good by buying hymn books for the church she would like to attend and all seemed happy as a marriage bell. Then, on the eve of the summer, word came that her lawyer had drawn all her funds and fled the country. She was ruined. She could not pay for*

> the things she had ordered or the servants. So as the party gathered she slipped away by train and was across to Boston before she could be located. Later she renewed her swimming exhibitions, married a suitable sugar daddy and lived to a ripe old age in California. But in the old memories of Annapolis Royal there lives the story of the big night when the hotel opened for business with all the pomp the area could muster—and there was no hostess.

The differences between the two accounts of Clara coming back to Annapolis Royal are intriguing and I could hear George positively chortling. His Sunday school teacher 'Lottie' was proving as unreliable as he remembered her. Then, George has done a lot of research on the deeds of Annapolis Royal, and found that Clara actually made a profit of $500 from her seven-month ownership when she sold her share of the house on the 13th of September, 1909.

The California reference proved reliable, as Clara did spend some years in the 1920s in Santa Monica, and implies that Charlotte somehow heard news of Clara over the years. I never found Clara taking up swimming exhibitions again but believe that I did eventually discover Clara's 'sugar-daddy' (as I explain in a subsequent chapter).

No wonder no one in Annapolis Royal remembers Clara! Or wanted to speak of her! Town policeman Conlin was asked on the 2nd of November, 1909 at Town Council why he had not arrested Mrs. McInnis, and that is the last reference we find to Clara and Annapolis Royal.

I knew the two gentlemen who had restored the 'Queen Anne Inn' in the 1980s, and queried them mercilessly about what Clara might have left behind. George also worked there one summer doing dishes, but I doubt that he ever got into the attic. If Clara left anything behind after her sudden departure, no one has recognized it

Bert Clarke died in 1950 and Charlotte Perkins in 1964. Both are buried at Woodlawn, and both took their memories with them.

George kept insisting that Bert Clarke would have kept a scrapbook, given that Clara was his protégée (and maybe more than that). Clarke is certainly the most plausible source for a scrapbook, and I followed up with anyone with memories of Clarke, even contacting his daughter and son. No one admits to any Bert-Clara memorabilia surviving, but maybe this report will prompt them to look again.

Clara was never to return to Annapolis Royal, as far as I know, and never again used the McInnis name, despite considerable money coming to her from the McInnis estate for the next 34 years.

It appears that Clara was always attracted to money—or money was attracted to her? In any case, Clara had other reasons for returning to New England that Charlotte and Annapolis Royal perhaps knew nothing of.

6: Mrs. Clement Miller

Somehow in his genealogical researches, George found a marriage certificate for Clara, as a widow from Brandon, Manitoba, marrying Clement G. Miller on the 25th of November, 1908 at People's Temple Methodist Church in Boston.

I was ready to denounce his foolishness because we knew that Clara had come to Annapolis in January of 1909 as the widow, Mrs. C. M. McInnis! He reminded me that the marriage license from 1908 identified Clara's parents as Manning Beckwith and Abbie J. Wade! Another improbable twist in 'pursuing Clara', but one that convinced both of us that Clara Sabean, Clara Beckwith, Clara McInnis and Clara Miller were one and the same person.

Clement Miller was a 41-year-old orchestra musician in Boston, maybe known to Clara from her performing years in Boston? On the marriage certificate, Clara claimed to be born in England and still retained her Beckwith name from her performing days. I am convinced that Clement Miller was the unidentified friend travelling with Clara to Annapolis Royal when she was opening the 'Old Orchard House' as an inn in the spring of 1909. And maybe "Old Annapolis Royal" was disconcerted by this wealthy widow having a 'gentleman friend'?

Clement had lived with his parents before he married Clara. The newlyweds rented 228 Huntington Street in Boston, according to the 1910 census. This was and is a fashionable and convenient address, and one has to wonder if Clara ever visited her old performing haunts or reconnected with any of her 'friends' from her earlier life.

Clement Miller enlisted as a private with the US 17th Infantry and apparently fought in the First World War. After the war, Clement returned to New England and worked as orchestra musician for the rest of his life. Clement Miller was listed as 'divorced' in the census records of 1920, 1930 and 1940, but I never did find a record of this divorce. Mind you, none of the genealogy sources are as good with documenting divorces as they are with marriages and births.

I also wondered if Clara reconnected with Caroline Hardwicke (her business partner in the 'Old Orchard Inn' investment) back in New England. Boston and Wellesley City Directories told me where Caroline was living and that she attained assistant professor rank at Wellesley College, but never afforded any hint of Clara.

If Caroline provided friendship when Clement Miller went to war or the marriage ran into trouble any ongoing connection ended when Caroline died of tuberculosis in 1919. Caroline had always maintained her connections to Nova Scotia and the *Annapolis Spectator* of March 6th, 1919 reported her passing:

> *A telegram was received last night announcing the death in Wellesley, Mass of Miss Carrie A. Hardwicke, daughter of Rufus W. Hardwicke of this town. She had visited here as usual during her vacation last summer when she always renewed old friendships and made new ones. Although not in robust health for some time her death was quite unexpected.*

Clement Miller died in 1948 at Tetland Masonic Home in New Hampshire, where he had connections for most of his life. Tetland appears to have been a rest home, causing me to wonder if Clement Miller had suffered from post-traumatic stress in WW I. I never could find an obituary for him, but Google came through with Clement Miller's only legacy, a 90-second piano score by a J. Fisher, 'Easy Pieces #5, An Old Court Dance', dedicated to him. I was delighted to challenge George with this, but he didn't have this piece in his formidable sheet music collection.

Then, maybe Clara reconnected with her family back in New England? Clara's mother and father never appear together in any record in the US, and by 1900 her mother was listed as widowed. The only hint I ever found of Clara connecting with her family in New England was the July 4th, 1889 *Boston Globe* reference to Clara spending the summer at a cottage with her mother and sister.

Clara's father died in 1899 and her mother in 1916. We have not found obituaries or headstones for either of them. Clara clearly would have had the means to provide for headstones and cemetery plots, and thus we can only assume that she had lost all connection with her parents over the years. Clara's younger sister "Annie" (presumably Nancy, based on the age of her birth), is buried at Mt. Hope Cemetery in Boston in 1908, perhaps suggesting that Clara was able to look after this.

It did take a few years for Clara's payments from the McInnis estate to be switched from Clara McInnis to Clara McInnis Miller in 1914 and to Clara Miller in 1915. Clara kept the 'Miller' surname for the rest of her life and was always listed as 'widowed' in the census reports.

Clara was clearly at a loss as Mrs. Clement Miller, but then she reconnected with someone from her previous self on that trip on the steamer 'Hunter' that brought her to New England, as impossible as that sounds.

Ernest J. Dick

7: Clara Miller

Next, George somehow found Clara as Clara Miller, living as a servant in the Tebbetts home at 37 Baltimore St. in Lynn, Massachusetts, according to the US census in January, 1920. Her age, 37, was as flexible as usual, and the report listed Clara as widowed. Clara claimed to be born in Maryland, which I knew she was now considering home. Her parents were said to born in England, which was what Clara had been claiming for 35 years now.

I was dubious that this was 'my' Clara. Genealogists can be inclined to 'wishful' connecting but I had to check out this 'find'.

The Tebbetts family was a 9th generation American founding family, built on shoe-manufacturing, and George was quick to remind me of many a Maritimer ending up in Lynn. The Tebbetts family also maintained properties back in England and travelled frequently between the old and new worlds.

Then Google's algorithms made a connection that no one could have invented! A newspaper report from July of 1923, printed in Los Angeles, Boston and New York papers, confirmed a most implausible relation between Clara and Theodore Tebbetts:

> *Mrs. Clara May Miller, saleswoman for an oil syndicate in Los Angeles, has announced receipt of a letter from a Boston law firm telling her she had been left $250,000 in the will of Theodore C. Tebbetts, leather manufacturer of*

> Lynn, Mass., who she saved from drowning when he was a small boy.
>
> About twenty-five years ago, Mrs. Miller said, she was a member of a party crossing the Bay of Fundy on a steamship. Tebbetts, then a precocious youngster, climbed on the railing and fell overboard. Mrs. Miller, then Miss Clara Beckwith, although fully dressed, jumped in to the sea and rescued the boy after a hard struggle.
>
> Young Tebbetts' father gave her $1,000 to buy clothes to replace those ruined in saving his son, she said.

Clara's very vivid story of saving the "youngster" in the Bay of Fundy in her 1893 'autobiography' came to mind (p.126), and the Tebbetts family could well have been vacationing in Nova Scotia. Clara's reward of $1,000 for saving the 16-year old Theodore was more than a usual reward (it would be worth over $25,000 today) and could well have 'obligated' Clara never to mention the name of the "youngster".

I had to learn everything I could about Theodore Tebbetts. He was born in 1871, and so was a year younger than Clara, and graduated from Harvard and Columbia Law School. He spoke several languages, travelled regularly to Europe and owned an estate on the Isle of Jersey. He was said to be a man of "fine ability", belonged to many clubs and in 1900 inherited the family business. How long Clara lived with the family I was never able to determine, despite challenging dozens of web-sites in dozens of different ways.

Clara was again keeping a very low profile and never made it into the social columns of local newspapers in Lynn. I did learn that she was living with the Tebbetts family when Theodore killed himself with a revolver on July 26th, 1920 "after several years of ill health and despondency". He had suffered two attacks of influenza in recent weeks and was said to be under the "care of a physician and nurse."[24]

Of course, most obituaries skirted around his cause of death, but concluding that he died of his own hand is unavoidable if anyone reads all of them.

His school yearbook obituary remembered Theodore Charles Tebbetts' "unfailing geniality and his delightful contributions in verse and song", which sounds very similar to what was said of Stanley McInnis after he died.

The July 1923 press notice of Clara potentially receiving $250,000 from the Tebbetts estate was reprinted in a many newspapers, and was immediately denounced by Mrs. Tebbetts. The widow first claimed that she knew nothing of Clara; then that Mr. Tebbetts never met Clara; but eventually conceded that Clara was a "good cook but discharged for other reasons."[25]

The evasiveness of Mrs. Tebbetts suggested for me that something suspicious may have been going on between Clara and her husband. Maybe I was watching too many crime and legal television shows, but I now had an explanation as to why Clara had never divulged the name of the lad she saved from drowning in the Bay of Fundy.

The $1,000 the Tebbetts family admitted that they had paid Clara could well have been paid for her silence, an agreement that she dutifully respected for 35 years. In Clara's 1893 'autobiography', the family travelling from Halifax could well have been the Tebbetts family. Certainly, it would have been scandalous for the Tebbetts family to even admit to their "youngster" being saved from drowning, and they certainly had the means to prevent press coverage of such a drama.

Maybe they were sending Clara far away to California in July, 1920, after the suicide of Theodore Tebbetts? George conceded that my construction of the confirmed evidence was plausible, and offered that Clara and Theodore could easily have met on the streets of Annapolis Royal while the Tebbetts family was waiting for their steamer 'Hunter' to take them home. Certainly a rail diversion between Halifax and Annapolis Royal between ships was possible, if you had sufficient resources and time on returning to America from Europe.

We further wondered if 17-year-old Clara and 16-year-old Theodore had become too 'attached' for the Theodore's parents' liking. Maybe the two of them had organized this 'life-saving', or perhaps the fall into the sea was an early attempt to commit suicide?

I researched Clara's reinventing herself in Los Angeles as "saleswomen for an oil syndicate", but never was able to find anything of her life here. The McInnis probate records do confirm that some of Clara's payments in the 1920s were sent to California, and Charlotte had told Will. R. Bird about Clara living in California.

Then George remembered that a small sum from the McInnis estate had gone to a step-mother in California, and suggested that Clara may have been staying with her. This was as plausible as Clara being a saleswoman for anything, but Clara's tenure in California never afforded further clues. George had lots of fun imagining what Clara could be up to in the California of the 1920s, but my archival instincts would not indulge these.

Maybe the affairs of the Tebbetts family would tell me something of Clara? I contacted the Lynn Museum and Historical Society, happily paying their research fee, as I expected them to have extensive files on the Tebbetts family. Theodore had been an early member of the Historical Society. However, all they could send me was the notice of his death and funeral, prompting me to wonder what they were not able to tell me. They did explain that the Tebbetts home on Baltimore Ave. had been torn down, meaning that I couldn't knock on the door to see Clara's room or her statue.

As for the Tebbetts fortune of $250,000 being claimed on Clara's behalf by a Boston law firm, we have found nothing beyond many newspapers publishing the same news report. Legal records, as with health records, rarely survive or become publicly accessible. Whether protecting the privacy of the client or patient, or the lawyer and physician, such records for Clara's story never came to light. I did try to interest more than a few legal friends on Clara's behalf, but none dared to venture into this territory. In the absence of proof, I do not believe that Clara got a further penny from the Tebbetts family once her "youngster" died in 1920.

Clara Miller did receive payments in California from the McInnis estate from 1925 through 1928, and perhaps in other years. Probate records are not consistent in explaining where payments were being sent. But we do know that Clara swore an affidavit in the offices of Norman Trippe, Forbush and Trippe of 53 State Street in Boston on the 26th of February, 1931. Apparently the Winnipeg firm administering the estate had questions about Clara and needed confirmation of her receiving the ongoing payments.

Following Clara in the 1920s, 30s and 40s became difficult. I checked out all the Clara Sabeans, Clara Beckwiths, Mrs. Clement Millers and Clara Millers that digital resources brought to light, though I know full well that fresh eyes with more digital savvy than myself might well find more.

I knew that Clara Beckwith considered Baltimore her home from her time there after 1893. She was reported as being from Baltimore when she visited Manitoba in November, 1897 and was said to be living at 926 North Fulton (an 1870 row-house in Baltimore) when the *Baltimore Sun* published her wedding announcement to Stanley McInnis in February of 1898.

Maryland was also listed as Clara Miller's place of birth in census records in 1920 and 1940, and on Clara's death certificate. Unfortunately, the Baltimore newspapers didn't cover Clara, or gossip about her, no more than did the papers in other centres where she performed. I have no evidence that Clara ever lived in Baltimore after 1898, and thus have to wonder what happened there for it to become 'home'.

I have come to a new appreciation for the old-fashioned census, and would greatly treasure a long-form census report for Clara, if they had existed in her day. Census reports are invaluable resources because they are mandatory and systematic, thereby well suited to robotic indexing once they are transcribed.

I was determined to find Clara in the US census every ten years, but 2,755 'Clara Millers" in 1930 and almost 21,000 for 1940 were more than I could check through. Adding her birth dates and middle initial M reduced the number to 344 for 1930 and 1,998 for 1940, but I couldn't be certain which birth date Clara might have given the census taker, or whether she was still using her middle name. Or maybe she avoided the census-taker altogether?

Finding Clara in the 1930 census was further complicated by not knowing when she might have returned to New England from California. I can offer my leads to anyone who wants to revisit them, but here George had no potential sightings for me.

For the 1940 census, I expected that Clara was back in the Boston area, because her death certificate told me she was here in 1943. This reduced the number of 'Clara Millers' to 12 whom I could methodically work through.

Here I found Clara, using her middle initial, 'M' and living and renting at the same address (79 Warren St) where she died three years later. Clara's address at 79 Warren was finally a concrete lead! In the 1940 census Clara was listed as widowed and head of the household, living in the same unit with two other women: Bertha Burgess, 56 and working as a nurse for a private family; and Eliza Morse, 84, from Nova Scotia.

Clara herself, now 66, was listed as working 52 weeks of the year (12 hours every day of the week) without remuneration as a nurse. Had Clara re-invented herself again...or was Clara having the census-taker on?

I did have a very reliable date of her death from the McInnis probate records: May 31, 1943. This let me order Clara's death certificate from the Department of Public Health, Registry of Vital Records and Statistics of the Commonwealth of Massachusetts.

Clara's medical history for her final decade was well-documented, implying that she had been under medical care for those 10 years. Her diabetic condition had apparently become cancerous in the last six months of her life and she died after being in a coma for a couple of days.

The most poignant and telling detail of Clara's death certificate was that Boston Public Welfare was listed as next of kin and informant for the Massachusetts Department of Public Health, implying that she was very poor. This was curious, as she should have been receiving her annual stipend from the McInnis estate.

I returned to the McInnis probate records and confirmed that her $1,000 a year annuity was still being paid. However, beginning in the mid 1920s, claims began to be paid to others on Clara's behalf, suggesting that Clara was not always paying her own bills. From this point on Clara's annual payment was paid to a Mrs. L. Merriam (1926), Siloon Merriam (1932-35), Myron P. Lewis (1936-38) and E. Larsen (1939-42). Then, in December, 1943 a final payment of $230 was made to E. Larsen and the balance of the McInnis estate was gifted to the Provincial Sanatorium.

Of course, I checked all these names. I found only Myron P. Lewis as Boston Park Commissioner, a prominent businessman and manager with a trust company. The others undoubtedly have their own family histories that may even have been researched, but George was not going to research further leads for me. He had his own families he was researching.

What was happening with Clara? George offered that Clara might have been mentally, emotionally, or physically incompetent to look after herself, and that welfare had stepped in. Certainly Clara's annual $1,000 could have been handsome compensation for Boston Public Welfare, and a sum they could not claim for other of their charges.

Clara's death certificate also told me that her remains were sent to Mt. Hope Cemetery in south Boston, but the death certificate knew nothing of Clara's mother or father. Clara's mother's death certificate told me she was buried at Mt. Hope in 1916, as was her sister Annie in 1908.

I promptly contacted the Mt. Hope Cemetery, and they easily gave me the location for Annie's grave (Section F–Grave 2214). Clara and her mother were buried in unmarked graves with the poor. No headstone was ever installed for Clara or her mother. The McInnis estate would undoubtedly have paid for a headstone, but no one was left to pursue such arrangements.

No obituary was ever written for Clara, and she was forgotten by everyone...except for Charlotte Perkins.

8: Pursuing Clara

Clara was clearly a precocious, athletic and exceptional person, ahead of her time. Clara reinvented herself more than once and was being reinvented—maybe both at the same time!

Clara needed a friend, partner, mentor, and lover, as we all do. Clara clearly had all of these, but always briefly, and they never seemed to have sustained her. Or maybe no one ever came to believe in Clara? Relationships invariably are mutual, with complications that forever confound us.

Clara's father abandoning the family for America when she was 15 or 16 was not unusual, though no less difficult for Clara for being the experience of many children. Then, Clara's mother had younger children she had to tend to. Certainly it made running away from Nova Scotia on the steamer 'Hunter' an obvious solution for Clara.

Clara connecting with a teen-age 'Theo/Teddy' Tebbetts, with all the Tebbetts' wealth and stature, was both brilliant and an act of desperation. Having Clara saving Theo's life in the waters of the Bay of Fundy would surely indebt the family to her, as indeed it did. Both Clara and Theo were clearly impetuous and adventurous enough to carry out such an adventure. I imagine them practising the rescue off the end of the Queen's Wharf in Annapolis.

Before Theo Tebbetts, I am convinced that Clara's first male relationship was with Bert Clarke. Their passion for swimming would have brought them together in Annapolis Royal in their early teens, and Clarke finding Clara's statue in Washington years later certainly suggests a lingering affection. Indeed, I imagine Clara and Bert Clarke reconnecting in 1908 when she came back to Annapolis Royal, but her 'friend' (Clement Miller) would have dissuaded Clarke from renewing his earlier affections.

Back in the late 1880s, Clara and Theo hadn't thought through what would happen next after Clara saved him from drowning, and the Tebbetts family could not allow for a continuing relationship between this run-away from Nova Scotia and their oldest son. They had to bring this to an end quickly and decisively, so they indentured or contracted her, or bribed George Lothrup at the Boston Grand Museum to take Clara on.

The $1,000 the Tebbetts family paid Clara might well have gone to Lothrup to 'keep' Clara far away from Lynn and their equally precocious son. I doubt that Clara ever got this reward, though Lothrop did give her fame, even if without the fortune. Indeed, I do not believe that Clara ever learned to manage her own finances, though a lot of money passed through her hands in her 73 years.

George Lothrup was clearly Clara's first manager...and probably much more. Her absence from the 1890 US census when she was at her performing peak is not surprising. She was an 'illegal immigrant', or at least 'unofficial'. I believe that Clara was kept at the 'Boston Grand Museum' so that Lothrop could use her as he saw fit. I imagine that Clara could have been pregnant in the twelve months she was away from public notice in 1892, and a miscarriage in these dubious circumstances could well have prevented Clara from ever having children thereafter.

Clara would naturally been scared, confused, grateful and thrilled with her life in the early 1890s in Boston. Even if she had read of Agnes Beckwith, she would not have had the remotest notion of anyone becoming 'world champion lady swimmer' or the 'world's most perfectly formed body', nor did anyone else. Clara's accomplishments were so far ahead of her time that no one took them seriously. These were inventions that the world had not seen, and inventing a competitive sport or a performance is as complicated and confusing as all other inventions always have been.

Clara clearly had a new manager or promoter from January, 1893 on, reflecting a break from any relationship with the 'Boston Grand Museum' and George Lothrup. Likely this was James L. Kernan, as he operated facilities in both Baltimore and Washington where Clara performed. Also, Kernan becoming a wealthy philanthropist, founding the James Lawrence Kernan Hospital in Baltimore, makes him an intriguing prospect for authoring or funding the writing of her 'autobiography'.

Publicly, Clara, from 1893 on, offers a holistic approach to her swimming and I imagine her personally adopting the philosophy of life reflected in her 'autobiography' and her article in the 1895 *Good Health* magazine. I hope for Clara that she found for herself the "new grace and beauty" attributed to her statue, 'The Diving Girl', but have no evidence to confirm this hope. I do imagine that her statue survives in a private collection somewhere in New England.

Clara marrying the aspiring dentist and public figure in Brandon, Manitoba and becoming Mrs. Stanley McInnis is strange, but no stranger than her becoming Clara Beckwith. And it speaks to Clara needing a strong partner and organizer in her life. How they might have met and become married is surely the stuff of great romance, but beyond my practical imagining.

Clara's absence from the gossip columns and social notes of Manitoba newspapers troubles me. She could have attended the dozens of events that Stanley McInnis was responsible for, even appreciating his efforts on stage. But lots of performers cannot retire graciously, and maybe Clara's inventive and unprecedented performing and competing was not acceptable in Brandon, Manitoba in the first decade of the 20th century—or in Annapolis Royal, for that matter.

Stanley McInnis organizing his finances so carefully that Clara never controlled his estate but received an annual stipend was not unusual, but also may have reflected his distrust of her financial acumen. And all the accounting of Clara's claims and expenses over the years in the Stanley McInnis probate records suggest that Clara's handling of money over those years was problematic.

More than likely, Clara became a recluse in Brandon, and maybe for the rest of her life. Since Stanley and Clara did not have children (she was only 27 when they married), I imagine her spending long hours on her favourite mare, 'Maud'.

But not having children interrupts a cycle of life, particularly in the early decades of the 20th century, and probably brought a profound sadness into Clara's life.

Clara aspiring to become a hotelier back in Annapolis Royal after Brandon was a very different direction, and potentially a very public life. But it didn't work out for Clara, though there was more to it than Charlotte's discrete explanations in 1924 ("The tourist season was slim that summer, not what she had anticipated" (p.172) or in the 1950s "that her lawyer had drawn all her funds and fled the country."[26]

Clara came back from away, as Maritimers almost always do, but staying is always more complicated than one imagines. Your former self reasserts itself, and there would have been lots of ghosts around to remind Clara of her beginnings.

Clara's 'quick' marriage to Clement Miller in 1908 absolutely implies that Clara and Clement had reconnected from their earlier lives—or had they perhaps even carried on a correspondence from 1897? Clement Miller never attained any stature in his life as an orchestra musician, and maybe Clara missed the notoriety and money of her life in New England and Brandon. Indeed, one can see a pattern in Bert Clarke, Theo Tebbetts and Stanley McInnis all being irrepressible and 'precocious' connections for Clara

Then World War I intervened, disrupting Clara and Clement's life as it did for so many. Clement continued playing within the discipline and structure of an orchestra long after the war, but maybe he couldn't be the husband Clara needed.

Clement considered himself divorced, but Clara always thought of herself as 'widowed'. Maybe Clara wanted to be married but Clement could not be? Nonetheless, Clara used the Miller name for the rest of her life.

Another loss for Clara had to be Carrie Hardwicke dying in 1919. Investing together in their inn for Annapolis Royal 15 months after Clara became a widow suggests a longer and deeper relationship than simply a business partnership. Indeed, the 'Old Orchard House' may well have been Caroline's brainchild, given her entrepreneurial bent; though Clara being older and widowed, with substantial financial backing, would have made her the more logical leader in this enterprise.

Perhaps losing Clement to the war and Carrie to tuberculosis in 1919 drove Clara to the Tebbetts household in Lynn, Massachusetts by 1920. I doubt that Clara had any family connections by that point, as she surely would have paid for her mother's tombstone when she died in 1916, as she had done for her sister in 1908, if she had been in contact with her mother.

Clara was not likely ever a cook in the Tebbetts household, though whether she was mistress, companion or blackmailer I do wonder. Clearly Clara had an emotional attachment to Theodore Tebbetts that his widow did not welcome. This meant that she had to be again 'sent away', and California was a long way away in 1920.

Clara finding a 'sugar daddy' in California, as Charlotte Perkins told Will R. Bird in the 1950s, is an intriguing possibility. Perhaps Charlotte had a note to this effect from Clara from California? George imagined Clara having great fun in and around Hollywood in the 1920s, and I do wish that I could have found the slightest shred of evidence to support this.

Clara returned to New England from California by 1931 and may have been living with the support of Boston Public Welfare from this point on. Certainly her annual probate payments never came to her directly after this point, reflecting her incapacity to look after herself.

Considering herself a nurse may have been Clara's final reinvention of herself.

Clara did have a true friend in Charlotte Perkins, even if it was an unlikely friendship, as the best friendships sometimes can be. If anyone in the old colonial capital of Annapolis Royal was going to be aghast and dismissive about Clara's exploits and misadventures, it would have been Charlotte. Rather, Charlotte's tellings of Clara's story, both in 1924 and the 1950s, are admiring and non-judgmental. Perhaps Charlotte envied Clara's 'chutzpa' in opening and running a hotel in Annapolis Royal, which Charlotte never got to do with her family establishment.

Maybe both Clara and Charlotte were feminists ahead of their time. Charlotte's Junior Reading Club, the Pickwick Club and the Imperial Order of the Daughters of the Empire were women-only organizations in which Charlotte and friends debated, performed, did visual art and organized their community. Clara challenging American women to be unafraid of water could well have been admired by Charlotte as brave and progressive. Maybe Charlotte herself swam off the old Queen's Wharf in Annapolis in her younger days—though she never admitted to it in writing. Finally, Charlotte being a spinster might well have given her a genuine understanding of Clara's 'difficulties' with men.

Charlotte telling Clara's story gave our girl from Granville Ferry a legacy that otherwise would have been lost. In that she was the truest friend Clara ever had.

Thank you, Charlotte!

Ernest J. Dick

Afterword

Pursuing Clara has taught me a lot after a lifetime of working with the past. As archivist and curator I always had to know the provenance for anything, but with Clara I have sought to move beyond being the fastidious archivist. I have tried to make sense of the confusing and partial evidence, and become detective even if not historian.

Pursuing Clara would never have happened without digital communications and I learned much about the opportunities they afford in accessing the past. Optical character recognition and automated searching algorithms have exploded our searching of historical newspapers, and led me to references for Clara that I would absolutely, otherwise, never have found. Similarly, transcribing and indexing of census reports and vital statistics allow for remote and inexpensive access that allowed me to follow Clara from my Granville Ferry vantage point.

An old habit of asking different reference librarians or archivists the same question I now brought to the World Wide Web. My laptop computer, of course, soon anticipated what I would be asking, and thus I asked friends, librarians, archivists what their computer would answer to my questions. This led me to important resources that I might never have found on my own, and I recommend this research strategy.

Digital communications can also afford us misplaced and unwarranted confidence in what we can know of the past. Tedious conventional searching of original sources always reminds us of the limits of what we can know of history. Human cataloguing is obviously biased and misleading, and limited in what could be catalogued. The overwhelming robotic and formula-based data now accessible invariably gives us a confidence that we never had when searching through card catalogues or archival-search aids.

The formulas of digital communications also led me to some curious destinations. EBay and Amazon obviously 'noticed' my repeated searching of Clara's 'autobiography' and offered me a hard-cover collector's edition at $1,500. It had a bright, more-colourful cover and I had to check it out because maybe somebody else was researching Clara? Nothing of the sort, as EBay and Amazon were apparently simply detecting a commercial opportunity here.

I wasn't certain whether to be flattered or dismayed that Amazon was offering a hard-cover collector's edition of Clara's 'autobiography', though I would love to connect with anyone who may have taken up the offer. Then, after Professor Day published his essays on all of the Beckwiths, the World Wide Web reissued the 1893 *In the Swim* under the title *Learn to Swim*—with more modest prices.

Once I knew when Clara was performing in Boston, I ordered the *Boston Globe* on old-fashioned microfilm for Clara's first six months in 1889, and read it through, just as I might have in pre-digital times. I found nuances, repetitions and incidental references that algorithms had decided I did not need. Digital communications are never comprehensive, despite how impressive and random their data may be.

Researching Clara was also going to take time with local historical societies, as they invariably have collections and local knowledge that never will be digitized or even systematically organized and catalogued. Their idiosyncratic and random preservation of heritage and documentary miscellanea tells stories ignored and forgotten by our provincial, state and national institutions. I have always contributed to, and volunteered with, local historical societies, and thus donate all potential royalties from the sales of *Pursuing Clara* to the Annapolis Heritage Society.

Historians have been curiously cautious about researching and understanding women performing and competing in water in the 19th century. Women in public in water were ignored until British historian Dave Day took notice of the Beckwiths, the first family of swimming. But North American historians of sport, feminism and performance have a decided reticence about Clara's admittedly-improbable accomplishments. I read everyone I could find, and contacted more than a few authors, and maybe this report will come to their attention.

Clara clearly contributed to the invention of endurance swimming competitions, water ballet or synchronized swimming and even water polo, though before anything of the sort was accepted or understood. Clara also now sounds like a pioneer in promoting swimming for good health, and I hope that eventually feminist history will include and celebrate her.

Given all the time that I spent with Clara, many encouraged me to become bolder and imagine who Clara was, what she was thinking, how she was feeling. Clara's story sounds like a film script when I introduce her anywhere, and she certainly invites further understanding.

Maybe this historical detective report will inspire and facilitate further imagining and re-inventions for Clara. Be my guest. I happily offer my permission and cooperation ahead of anyone so doing, and will be pleased to read your first draft. And I promise to attend your book launch or the premiere of your film!

Clara fulfilled the old adage that truth is stranger than fiction, and that may be the most profound lesson I learned from her. I am of a generation very much encouraged to know and follow my own truth. Then my 75 years and digital communications has focused and emboldened my truth in recent years.

But Clara's truth truly has discombobulated everything, and may bring my career as detective of history to a close. My next project is a memoir: "Following all the Stories the Past has to Offer".

Thank you, Clara...and good-bye, Clara.

Ernest J. Dick,
September, 2020
Granville Ferry, Nova Scotia

Appendix A: *In the Swim*

Figure 4: The cover of Clara's 'autobiography'

Ernest J. Dick

Introductory

I have been asked to write my Autobiography, and to include therein a simple explanatory treatise upon the subject of swimming. From careful observation and investigation, aquatic sports are, unfortunately, too much neglected and indifferently considered on this side of the Atlantic. Without egotism or "self-praise," which the adage says is "half scandal," I believe that I can justly claim the privilege of speaking authoritatively upon aquatic subjects, swimming, especially. My sole purpose in at all consenting to write my Autobiography as a swimmer, is to encourage an art that within itself embodies the highest order of physical culture, not only largely contributing to the retention of perfect health, but likewise affording so many opportunities for rational and enjoyable diversion. If, in the recital of my experiences as a swimmer, I can arouse sufficient interest to encourage American girls to follow the example of their English cousins, I shall deem my efforts amply rewarded.

CLARA BECKWITH

Ernest J. Dick

The Land of my Birth

Having been authoritatively informed that I was born in Lambeth, England, October 26th, 1867, I have long since accepted that assurance with passive resignation, and incidentally refer to this most important event in my life's history, only because I believe it to be a wise and excellent idea, when a task is undertaken, to commence right at the beginning. From my earliest recollection. "T, Vater" has been my paramount thought. Long before I cherished the remotest idea of entering the field of professional swimmers, I could, as the saying goes, "swim like a duck." It must, however, be understood that I use the above quotation only in a comparative sense, because to swim absolutely like a duck would undoubtedly prove a disastrous venture for ordinary mortals. In my present condition of proficiency and confidence as an expert, pardon me for asserting that I can now swim BETTER THAN A DUCK.

During my professional career the press has generously conferred upon me many unique, but suggestive titles. among them, "*The Modern Mermaid,*" "*Neptune's favored daughter,*" "*The Water Nymph,*" and "*Naiad of the deep.*" I am grateful for the fact that my nature is not susceptible to flattery otherwise the success I have attained might have proved a question of serious doubt.

Naturally I am proud of the distinction of being recognized as the "*Champion Lady Swimmer of the World*," but my pride exists alone in the truth that my honors have been acquired by perseverance, hard work, and a determination to win unquestionable success in my life's vocation.

> "*Act well your part, there all the honor lies.*"

Swimming as an art or as an amusement is strangely neglected. Every man and every boy should be able to swim—for who knows how soon the art may be called into operation for the saving of life, your own or that of another. And if swimming be useful and desirable for men and boys, why not also for women and girls? Go in the summer season to any watering-place you like, and for one bather who can swim, you will see twenty who are content to paddle in the shallows afraid to go a foot out of their depth. They have no distaste for the water, evidently; but they cannot swim; and hence are in danger from every wave.

Ernest J. Dick

"LIKE FATHER, LIKE SON."

The desire and the ability to swim was born within me. My father, *William Manning Beckwith. of Lambeth*, England, maintained his position as Champion Swimmer of England for ten consecutive years, and only surrendered his well earned and amply deserved honors, when the vigor and vital forces of life were on the ebb, and he realized that his physical strength could be utilized to a more practical and consistent purpose. The title of CHAMPION then devolved upon my brother *William—"Like father, like son"*—for he has successfully defended it up to the present time. The professional careers of my father and brother have been a continued succession of triumphs. In their many contests with noted swimmers, in which the conditions included almost every imaginable test of skill and endurance, they never experiei1ced a single defeat. My younger brother, *Charles*, is also an excellent swimmer, but having no inclination nor ambition to become a professional expert, he swims just because he likes it and it comes natural. My sister Agnes, however, is an expert of high order, she has a record of swimming nine miles in the ocean, which remarkable feat is equal in exhaustion of energy, phys1cal force and powers of endurance, to swimming fifteen miles in placid waters. This incidental reference to my family is given only because it has direct association with the days of my childhood, when the all-prevailing and never-ceasing home topics were "swimming," "swimmers," "swimming races," and "swimming exhibitions." Figuratively speaking, I was constantly "*in the swim*," and have been in it ever since.

MY FIRST PUBLIC APPEARANCE.

Having passed the days of my childhood under influences that developed but one earnest and innate thought, I naturally became deeply absorbed in the subject of swimming. I grew ambitious to distinguish myself in what I then believed to be the greatest and grandest accomplishment in the world. It must be remembered, that at this period I was but a mere child, scarcely 12 years of age. In the simplicity of thought I permitted my imagination to picture just such scenes and triumphs as have, under the process of natural evolution, been actually experienced. At first my ambition was modest, I desired only to equal the skill and proficiency attained by my sister, and to accomplish in the art of swimming

, results only equal to her success. I had never taken a lesson in swimming, and yet with a confidence born of intuition, I boldly entered the water at the beach near my home and "*struck out*" for *fame and glory*. I started with the "chest stroke," and was not at all surprised to realize that I could swim almost without effort. It came natural.

Figure 5: The Chest Stroke

My first public appearance occurred in England when I was but 13 years of age. My father was present and witnessed my exhibition. It was then he predicted that some day I would be recognized as the "*Champion Lady Swimmer of the World.*" Under his fostering encouragement, I determined to adopt swimming as the vocation of my life, and if possible to verify my father's flattering prediction.

I issued daring challenges to all professional female swimmers. In my absolute confidence, strengthened by the applause so liberally bestowed by the multitudes who had witnessed my first aquatic efforts, I could not resist the inclination to deem myself invincible, and under the inspiration of that belief I resolved to make a severe and vigorous test of my skill. My challenges issued in England were not accepted, notwithstanding the fact that they were personally authoritative, and continued in full force and effect for nearly two years. The title of Champion was then conceded to me, but with only limited opportunity to prove that it was justly merited.

IN THE LAND OF THE FREE.

Failing in my efforts to arrange for a contest, in England, I bade a long adieu to the dear ones at home; said farewell to Lambeth and its fond associations, came to America about eleven years ago, and established my resid-

Ernest J. Dick

ence in Boston. Having fairly won a reputation *"on the other side of the Atlantic"* as the *"World's Champion Lady Swimmer,"* my arrival in America soon became widely heralded, and the announcement of my challenges promptly disclosed my purpose. Two long and anxious years elapsed ere an opportunity for a swimming contest was offered. My challenge was then accepted by Miss St. John. the conditions were to swim (against time) over a three and a-half mile course, from Little Orchard Island to Fort Independent and return. Miss St. John proved to be a clever, strong swimmer, but my greater muscular development and endurance enabled me easily to defeat her. Some months later a novel match was arranged. It was a six days' contest. My opponents were six professional lady swimmers, *each to swim only one day*, whilst I engaged to swim every day, contesting against them individually, and to singly swim more miles in the six days of the match than the total miles accomplished by my six opponents. The swimmers were Misses Cora Rogers, Annie Fern, Bertha Goodwin, Anna McVeigh, Kate Anderson, and Mary Roberts. The total number of miles accomplished by the six ladies above mentioned was 63¾. My record was 74:½ miles. I could have added five miles to my score, but the conditions of the race did not justify the extra exertion.

Pursuing Clara

SHE'S DROWNING! SHE'S SINKING!

My sextuple victory as described in the preceding chapter, of course, added prestige to my name and fame. My confidence increased, my challenges were now couched in more defiant terms than ever. I made the art of swimming a life study, and became so proficient in-various aquatic manipulations on the water's surface, that the greatest difficulty I experienced was to sink or keep myself under the water. During my leisure hours I practised many original swimming feats, and finally conceived the idea to include in my exhibitions a vivid and realistic representation of the struggles of a drowning person. After a few private and exclusive experiments, I was prepared to startle the people and determined to make my illustration as exciting as possible. Of course, my purpose was unknown. A great crowd had assembled to witness what had been advertised as a novel exhibition of aquatic sports. After successfully performing several of my most difficult feats, I suddenly gave a despairing cry, assumed a confused and distressed expression, and after a brief and seemingly hopeless struggle, I permitted myself to sink gain coming to the surface, my struggles became more pronounced, I heard the bustle of excitement among the spectators. "She's drowning! She's sinking! Get a rope!" Several gentlemen had removed their coats and vests, preparatory to my rescue. I then thought the commotion had lasted long enough; so assuming the easy and restful position of floating, I smilingly waved my compliments and thanks to the astounded multitude. When the good-natured spectators realized that it was all a hoax and that they had been cleverly "sold," I was gratified to hear their cordial shouts of approval.

After waiting patiently for additional acceptances of my challenge by female swimmers, I finally and reluctantly concluded there were none who desired to oppose me, I then arranged a six days' race with LEAVITT, the Champion Swimmer of Lowell, Mass. To my surprise and disappointment Leavitt retired from the contest after the first day. He was a fair swimmer, but lacked rapidity of movement and the enduring powers so essential to all professionals. Since my contest with Leavitt my claim to the title of *Champion Lady Swimmer of the World* has been undisputed, and is conceded by all male and female professionals.

SAVING HUMAN LIFE.

THREE RESCUES FROM DROWNING.

During the past few years I have been giving exhibitions in Boston, Lowell and throughout the New England States. A feature of my exhibition at Peak's Island, Portland, Maine, was diving from the upper deck of a moving steamer, a distance of nearly fifty feet, to the water. For a few moments I was lost to view in the foamy surging waves, but not for an instant did I lose presence of mind or confidence in the success of my venture. I solemnly realize that my health, strength, agility and powers, as a professional swimmer, are given to me by my Supreme Master, and I am grateful that through His Divine will I have been instrumental in saving the lives of three drowning persons. These rescues have repaid me a thousand fold for the years of hard work and effort to perfect myself in the art of swimming. My combined accomplishments as an expert swimmer are as nothing compared with the happy satisfaction I experience in. the knowledge that with God's aid, I have saved human life.

THE THREE RESCUES.

Ernest J. Dick

I was a passenger on the steamer "Hunter," crossing the Bay of Fundy. The steamer was speeding in rough waters at the rate of thirteen knots an hour. A storm seemed imminent. I was on the upper deck, enjoying the awe-inspiring aspect, a little child was leaning over the steamer's low guard-rail. There were at least twenty passengers on deck watching the gathering of dark and threatening clouds. I had casually noticed the "youngster," and was about to retire to the cabin.

Figure 6: No time could be lost

Pursuing Clara

As I turned toward the stairway. the steamer lurched heavily. and the child dashed headlong over the rail into the seething waters. In an instant I realized the situation: If it were possible to save the child, it must be done quickly. No time could be lost in removing skirts. Commending myself to the care and protection of Providence, I leaped overboard and was soon by the side of the drowning boy. My water-soaked skirts somewhat impeded my rapid progress, but my skill and physical powers proved masters of the trying situation. I sustained the child above water fully twenty minutes before assistance could be rendered. The steamer stopped, then backed, and when near enough a boat was quickly lowered and we were rescued, or rather I should say the child was safe. He proved to be the son of parents who were enjoying their vacation at Halifax, N. S.

—

I was enjoying a quiet and social stroll in company with a friend, at Crescent Beach, Mass., when my attention was attracted by the shouts of a crowd of men gathered upon a floating raft near the shore. Some distance beyond the raft I observed an elderly man struggling in the water. In an instant I realized that he was drowning and was already in

Ernest J. Dick

that dazed and bewildered condition, which is a sure indication of loss of self-control. I waded in until the water was deep enough to permit me to swim. A few swift strokes brought me within reaching distance of the struggling man, when, without ceremony or apology, I seized him vigorously by the hair. In return for my good intentions, the old gentleman grasped me by the throat, and it was only by the exercise of my utmost physical strength that I forced him to relax his hold. It was the clutch of a drowning man. The strain upon me was terrible, The weight of my drenched skirts served only to increase my difficulty in effecting the rescue. I finally succeeded in towing my prize to shallow water and in another moment had him safely on the beach.

—

On the pier at a famous summer resort I was enjoying the salt air breezes one charming day near the hour of twilight. The pier extended far out from the beach and was popularly appreciated as a cool and inviting promenade. In the midst of a merry group of young ladies, there suddenly occurred a commotion, heightened by several piercing shrieks. My intuition instantly advised me that some one bad fallen from the pier. The surf was heavy, and at that distance from the beach the undercurrent was strong and exceedingly dangerous. The victim in this instance was a boy, probably not more than fourteen years of age. He sank almost as soon as he touched the water. Without considering the possible consequences, I plunged (skirts and all) into the great sea of waves, and exerting my utmost strength and efforts I succeeded in reaching the child just as he was about to disappear for the third time. It was only after a most desperate struggle that I reached *terra firma* safely with the now-unconscious lad. He was soon revived, I never saw him on the pier again.

THE PHYSICAL CULTURE
—AND—
HYGIENE OF SWIMMING.

It is my earnest wish in reciting incidents of my "life in the water," to consistently avoid all semblance of egotism and self-laudation. This endeavor I find to be the greatest obstacle in giving intelligent and truthful illustrations of the varied experiences I wish to relate. The subject of swimming has been my all absorbing thought. To me it seems boundless, inexhaustible. It is no exaggeration to assert that

Ernest J. Dick

I am perfectly contented and "at home" in the water. I love its cooling, bracing and invigorating influences, and should I fail to experience its refreshing pleasures even for a single day, I would almost deem that day a blank in my existence. Among the greatest benefits I have derived from swimming is the remarkable preservation of my health in all seasons, and under all conditions of changing climate, diet and surroundings. It is, therefore, not surprising that I claim the art of swimming, or rather the ability to swim, as the highest type of physical culture. During the past eleven years I have not experienced a day's sickness. I therefore most enthusiastically urge upon my sex the importance of adopting swimming as a method of physical development. It is not necessary that you should engage to become a "champion," or even an expert swimmer.

The benefits to be derived from a: reasonable and consistent practice of the aquatic art are immeasurable. It is a remarkable truth that when natural timidity, fear and undue nervousness are overcome, and we gradually acquire the spirit of self-reliance and courage, we become brave and courageous in all things. It is the inspiration of self-confidence that seems to cling to us through life, as a direct result of increased vital force, and a perfectly healthful condition of mind and body. I sincerely believe that if every girl would learn to swim and practice it daily, or whenever a convenient opportunity presented itself, that there would be no necessity for any other system of physical training for women. As an exercise, it brings into motion every muscle of the body, making them yielding and expansive. and daily developing the natural powers of endurance. My only physical exercise has been and is that of swimming. The result is that I do not know what it is to be ill. My present weight is 1S6 pounds; my height 5 feet, 4 inches, and without any great exertion or straining I can lift a dead weight of 200 pounds.

A FEW INCIDENTAL COMMENTS.

The water in the swimming pool or aquarium, in which my exhibitions are usually given, is heated to a temperature of 92°. On retiring from the pool I go at once to my dressing room, which is heated several degrees greater than the water's temperature. When dressed, I am ready to "*go out doors*" in the coldest weather without experiencing any result save increased vigor and a remarkable bouyancy of health. It has been a matter of surprise to me to observe that there are so few conveniences in America for practicing swimming. It is no exaggeration to assert that in England fully three fourths of womankind can swim. They appear to encourage the practice as a gymnastic exercise. There are numerous public and private baths, also swimming pools connected with public and private schools, open the entire year. The beneficial results are so self-evident that no other argument in favor of swimming as a means of physical culture is deemed necessary.

HINTS TO BEGINNERS.

Don't try to learn swimming at the ocean beach, the seashore, nor where the surf is heavy.

Take your first lessons in a swimming pool or natatorium where the facilities and surroundings are safe.

Seek first of all to gain confidence, and do not attempt "the strokes" until you realize that you're not afraid of the water.

A timid person, who from any cause becomes nervous or unduly excited, is apt to encourage "cramps."

When you become used to the water and feel the inspiration of self-confidence, then you are in condition learn the chest stroke, upon which devolves the prime and fundamental principle of swimming, and which must be acquired before any other stroke, or manipulation is attempted. I employ the chest stroke in performing such feats as turning somersaults under the water, and in swimming with one leg out of the water. The chest stroke will be more fully explained in my general comments on swimming. Just here I shall merely add that it expands the chest and lungs and strengthens the wrists and shoulders.

SWIMMING IS EASY TO LEARN.

There is no difficulty in learning how to swim. It is almost as easy to float as to sink; and a little practical knowledge would prevent any man or boy from sinking. The one great requisite is confidence. That acquired, all the rest is comparatively easy.

It is almost as natural for a man as it is for a dog to swim. The one indispensable requisite is a confident belief that you cannot sink while you keep your hands under water and your legs the least in motion. You must begin at the beginning, in this as in everything else.

All animals swim without effort. They use the same, or almost the same, action in swimming as they do in walking or running. Man, however, has to use a kind of action in water impossible to him on land.

Ernest J. Dick

DON'T BE AFRAID.

The only obstacle to improvement in this beneficial and life-preserving art is fear; and it is only by overcoming this timidity that you can expect to become a master of the art. It is very common for novices in the art of swimming to make use of corks or bladders to assist in keeping the body above water. These may be of service for supporting the body while one is learning what is called the stroke, or that manner of drawing in and striking out the hands and feet that is necessary to produce progressive motion. But you will never swim until you can place confidence in the power of the water to support you; I would, therefore, advise all beginners to acquire that confidence first of all, especially as I have known persons who have, by a little practice necessary for that purpose, learned the stroke without knowing it. The practice I refer to is to select a place where the water deepens gradually, walk slowly into it till it is up to your breast, then face the shore. To encourage yourself to do this calmly, reflect that your progress will be from deep to shallow water, and that at any time you may raise your head far above the water by bringing your legs under you and standing on the bottom. Now plunge under with your eyes open. In this attempt you will find that the water buoys you up, and that it is not so easy to sink as you imagine. Thus, you will appreciate the supporting power of the water, and learn to confide in that power.

PRESENCE OF MIND.

I think I shall satisfy you that your body is lighter than water, and that you might float in it a long time with your mouth free for breathing, if you would place yourself in proper position, keep still and forbear struggling.

If a person unacquainted with swimming, and falling accidentally into the water, could have presence of mind sufficient to avoid struggling and plunging, and to let the body take a natural posture, he might continue safe from drowning till help should come.

I would not advise you, or any one, to depend on having this presence of mind on such an occasion, but learn fairly to swim, as I wish all were taught to do in their youth. You would then on many occasions, be safer for having that skill, and free from painful apprehensions of danger, to say nothing of the enjoyment of swimming as a delightful exercise.

Ernest J. Dick

SLOW AND STEADY IS THE RULE.

Plain swimming is a perfectly easy and simple operation. Keep your hands open, with the palms rather concave and the fingers close together, so that no water can pass through them. Now lean with your chest on the water, and as you throw your arms forward your body will assume a horizontal position, just beneath the surface. With slow and steady action let the legs. follow the motion of your arms, or rather, act simultaneously with them. Then spread the hands so as to describe a half-circle, the elbows coming close to the body, and then to the chest. A few yards is all you will accomplish at first. If you feel any inconvenience by the water entering your mouth, close your lips, and it cannot get in. As you progress, the management of the breath will cause you neither trouble nor anxiety, just keep your head up, hold your body straight, your limbs extended and your breath will take care of itself. Slow and steady is the rule in learning; swiftness will be certain to come with practice.

DON'T LOSE YOUR NERVE.

Keep your head well up, and, in getting ready for each successive stroke, draw back the legs by a simultaneous motion. Keep the feet wide apart, with the toes well turned out; and as you send out the arms kick the legs backwards and sideways to their full extent, keeping them separate till they have described as wide a circle as possible, the legs coming close together at the end of each stroke. Press against the water with the sole of the foot and not with the toes, and you will make more easy and rapid progress.

  If the young swimmer be at all nervous, he should get assistance from a friend. A good assistant will be found in a heavy plank on which the beginner may rest his hands occasionally, and so sustain himself, or push it before him as he proceeds. There is no necessity for going out of your depth, for great depth of water is not necessary for ordinary plain swimming.

AVOID RASHNESS AND TIMIDITY.

First of all. let me tell you that swimming cannot be taught on paper.

Ernest J. Dick

In choosing a bathing place, the swimmer should avoid deep ponds, reedy and weedy streams and rapid rivers, he must equally avoid excitement, rashness and timidity. His best plan is to go with a friend, and take 'his first lesson without hurry or anxiety.

In taking your first dip, walk quietly into the bath until the water is about up to your waist. Then paddle about till you get thoroughly accustomed to what we may call the "feel" of the water. This will give you confidence, and you will soon become aware of the fact that your body is lighter than the water it displaces, and that it has a constant tendency to lift you off your feet.

Now is the time to "*take a duck*," so as to thoroughly immerse yourself. Rise without hurry or nervousness and turn your face to the shore. Bring your hands together, palm to palm, and attempt your first stroke by spreading them outwards, and at the same moment throw the legs wide apart. An excellent plan is for a friend or instructor to place his hand just under the pupil's chest. This gives him confidence. He will soon learn that he can sustain himself in the water without assistance, which means that he can swim.

PERSEVERE AND YOU WILL SUCCEED.

In your first attempt, you will do little more than kick your legs and arms about, and perhaps make a stroke or two; in a few days, however, you will become bolder and perhaps make three, four, or half-a-dozen strokes. Persevere and you will succeed. A little assistance from a friend's hand, occasionally, under the chin or the chest will be useful.

The first to learn is a strong, steady stroke. This will be best accomplished by means of the chest stroke. The swimmer throws himself upon the water and leans upon it, with his chest, at the same time keeping his feet wide apart and as near the surface as possible without actually allowing them to be above water. The hands should he open, of course, but the fingers and thumb should all be close to each other so as to hold the water, much in the way the blade of an oar holds it in the act of rowing. The whole body should be kept as flat and as straight as possible, the strokes taken without hurry or splash.

Of course, there are many who will never become swimmers, try as hard as they may. I have seen many a mature-looking individual hopping about with one leg on the bottom while making frantic movements with the arms, and never accomplishing a single stroke, Such people never get over the initial step.

SWIMMING ON THE BACK.

Perhaps the easiest way of supporting the body in the water is to float, or to swim on the back. Easy, that is, after the method is once acquired. *"The water washing over my face,"* says a friend, describing the operation, *"somewhat frightened me at first, and I floundered about a good deal, waving my arms and filling my mouth with water. But I soon overcame my difficulty. Standing with my face to the bank, I drew up my legs, and placing them against it, pushed myself off into the stream, keeping my arms close to my sides."*

The beginner should keep bis bead to the billows, so as to rise and fall with them, otherwise the water may wash in a disagreeable manner over the face, as it did over mine. In fresh water it is not so easy to float; rather more exertion is required.

In swimming on the back the position is the same as that in floating, except that the arms need not be stretched out. Keep the toes well turned out and the hands perfectly still and close to the sides, and you will find that you will not sink, though the water will come half over your face.

Figure 7: Swimming on the Back

FLOATING IS EASY.

Floating is not by any means difficult if you can lie on your back without struggling. Keep your body as straight as you can, your chest well up, your arms extended, or stretched back over or under your head. Very little movement of the limbs will keep the body on the top of the water, with just the face, the chest, and tops of the knees above.

Figure 8: Floating

Being able to float a little and make a few strokes, you will by this time make the plunge without fear.

TAKING A "HEADER."

Pursuing Clara

The plunge is a safe and effectual way of entering the water, though at first it is just a little startling.

If, however, you bend too much forward, you will probably turn a somersault. When you arr. in the water straighten the limbs, and you will almost immediately rise to the surface.

The header can be made from almost any height. J. B. Johnson, the professional swimmer, made it from a parapet of London Bridge, and got a "booming" editorial in a morning paper for his daring.

Of course, the faculty of diving from a height into the water is only to be acquired by long practice. The professional swimmers are. all adept at this feat; and a very inspiring and thrilling feat it is.

In rising to the surface all you have to do is to raise your hands and strike downward with your feet; lea ping · in fact, to the surface. By merely keeping still, however, and letting the body be upright, you will come to the surface, though not so rapidly.

The depth to which you descend will, of course, depend on the amount of force employed in making the dive, the length of the run and the power of the dash. You need not be afraid of the depth; for there is no more danger in twelve fathoms of water than there is in two. If you once acquire the confidence necessary to dive, you will be under no apprehension about coming to the surface again.

Figure 9: Diving, or Taking a Header

PLAIN CHEST SWIMMING.

Keep both legs and arms in almost simultaneous motion. The heels should be drawn up to almost touch the body, and then struck outright and left, precisely as though you were going to kick in opposite directions. Bring the feet together again, and at the same time make a wide and forward sweep with the hands.

To lessen the resistance of the water, point the toes downwards and keep the hands flat. In plain swimming you have to get all the support you can from the water; and by keeping the hands flat you necessarily increase the resting surface.

Reach out with the hands as far as you can, and avoid the jerking motion you are unconsciously likely to fall into. Remember, also, that the main principle of swimming is steadiness and power. Rapidity will come with practice. Steadiness and endurance must be the first requisites of the young swimmer.

Good; strong, steady, chest swimming is that which all beginners should practice; the chest-stroke first; the side-stroke when you are quite proficient. We must all walk before we can run. Running is very useful sometimes, but steady walking accomplishes greater distances.

SIDE AND OVERHAND STROKES.

There are two practical styles of side swimming, known as the side-stroke and the overhand. In both, the swimmer is on his side, and is able to make great progress in consequence of the less resistance offered by his body.

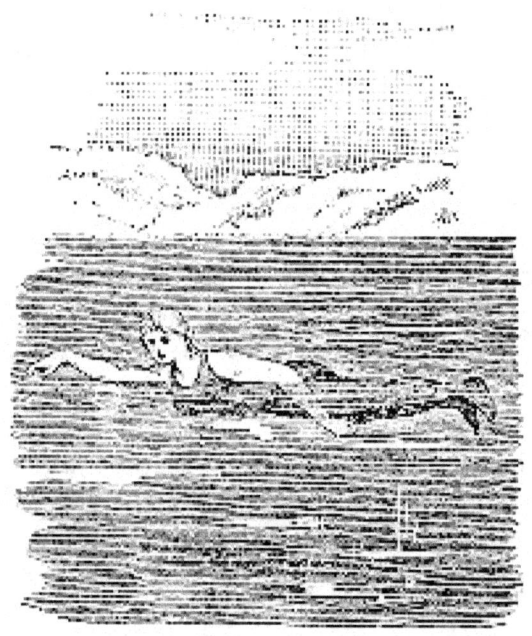

Figure 10: The Overhand Stroke

In swimming competitions the side-stroke is very popular, as by it more rapidity is attained than by the regular breast-stroke. There is, also, in it an air of considerable grace and power of movement.

Presuming that the learner can go on for a quarter of an hour without stopping with the regular chest-stroke he may then commence side swimming. This is the plan: Lay the face and body well down sideways in the water, with the mouth a little raised to enable you to breathe freely. Except the upper half of the face and the top of the shoulder the whole body is under water. It matters not which side you swim on, though most swimmers can go faster on one side than the other. The method of progress is precisely the same. The upper hand is used as a sort of cut-water, and with each stroke sent out as far as possible, the other hand resting on the side, or only brought occasionally into use as a rudder to steady the body. The legs are employed in the same way as in breast swimming, care being taken not to allow the upper leg to come above the surface.

The chief difficulty in side swimming is the management of the breath; for as the arm goes forward and downward, there is always a tendency for the head to sink lower and lower. The professional swimmer, to obviate this keeps his body as straight as possible, and occasionally gives his head a sort of wrench, as though to shake it free from the water.

Figure 11: The Side Stroke

The method of proceeding is this: First, lift one hand out of the water, and swing the whole arm and shoulder through the air, with a sweep as far as possible in advance of the head. Then drop the arm sideways into the water, the palm of the hand downwards. It will be found, that the shoulder being so far advanced, the body is thrown on its side the instant the hand reaches the water, and the opposite leg having been drawn up will be thrust back and the body propelled through the water.

Figure 12: Swimming Without Using the Arms

Then move the extended arm backwards towards the hip, and when straight with it, raise it towards the water and repeat the swinging action of the arms and shoulder as before.

Ernest J. Dick

The swimmer seems to be hurled forward with every sweep of the arm, and as stroke succeeds stroke, it seems as though he were successively trying to seize something in front of him and drag himself along. Of course, the legs must be employed as in regular chest swimming; the only difference being that one is higher up in the water than the other, and is apt to come upon the surface and waste its strength in the air.

This method—and, indeed, any method—cannot be taught in a book. It must be practised in the water; and the practice must be constant.

Swimming on the side is a pleasant and agreeable change from breast swimming. There is no need to attempt any particularly rapid action. Fast swimming, as I have already said, is much less important than endurance, and must not be forced.

SWIMMING UNDER THE WATER.

Whoever has witnessed a public swimming-match will have noted one very remarkable fact, namely, that nearly as much swimming takes place below as upon the surface.

Swimming under water is as easy, or perhaps more easy than swimming on the surface. The method employed is precisely the same; and when the disagreeable feeling of total immersion is overcome, the plan is quite easy.

Good practice in diving will soon make the amateur so familiar with the water as to enable him to do almost anything he likes. To accustom yourself to the sensation of holding the breath under the surface, dip your head into a basin, and hold the face below while you mentally count from one to a dozen. Practice this frequently, and you will soon find that the time of immersion can be increased from a few seconds to a minute or more. You need not shut your eyes, though the natural tendency is to do so. When retaining your breath becomes painful. raise your head out of the water, inhale the air fully and rapidly, and repeat the experiment.

Combined with the breast-stroke, the side-stroke, and the hand-over-hand-stroke, the swimmer may relieve himself by paddling like a dog or by imitating the frog—though, as I have already said, the imitation is, at best, but a poor one.

Do not be discouraged by failure. Persevere daily in all the styles, and you surely will succeed. I do not pretend that every learner will become an accomplished swimmer; but certainly in a short time he will learn enough to guarantee for himself, the enjoyment of this healthful and delightful exercise.

Figure 13: Swimming Under Water

HOW TO TREAD WATER.

Every swimmer should be able to Tread Water. By this term is understood the capacity for standing upright in the water and keeping the head above the surface. It is done thus: Lower the limbs full length, and raise the hands just to the top of the water; then tread downwards with the feet flat, as in going up a

Pursuing Clara

flight of stairs or exercising on a treadmill. I don't suppose that any of my readers have had the latter experience, but most of them know the sort of action necessary-a continual treading and stepping without progression.

Figure 14: Treading Water

The toes should be kept closed to prevent the water passing between them. A slight movement of the hands on the surface will assist the treader in keeping upright. In this position you can remain some time, and by swaying the body a little to the right or the left, some slight progress may be made. You know the joke about a man being Webb-footed; well, perhaps, if a man were to put on a pair of thin, broad-soled shoes, or, better still, a pair of Canadian snow shoes, he might be better able to Tread Water more gracefully.

Balancing—A modification of the method of treading water is useful when out of your depth and you wish to take a little rest. It requires confidence, but it is not difficult of accomplishment. Lower your feet full length, let your head fall gently back till your chin is just level with the surface. The farther back the head is, the more perfect will be the balance. Some swimmers in this position can fold their arms and cross one foot over the other; but the general plan is to hold the arms under the water close to your sides, and merely turn the hands a little, like fins or paddles. The body must otherwise be quite at rest. When you wish to assume the horizontal position, raise your arms above your head and, at the same instant, give your feet an upward turn. In an instant you will be able to resume the ordinary float or to turn upon the breast and swim.

WALKING ON MY HANDS
UNDER THE WATER.

Seemingly one of my most difficult aquatic acts is that of walking on my hands in the water, with the body extended upward, and feet projecting above the surface. This feat of course requires care and precision, but is otherwise easy. I am sure that I can walk upon my bands more skillfully, and with greater comfort, in the water than out of it, because the water materially assists in balancing the body. In performing this and other "under the water" feats, I keep my eyes open in order to see exactly where I am going and to avoid any object that might impede my progress.

Figure 15: Beckwith Walking on her Hands

Ernest J. Dick

HOW TO RESIST CRAMPS.

Swimmers are exposed to a muscular contraction which is known by the name of cramps—a contraction which renders powerless the limb it attacks. It is not necessary to be frightened at "cramps," as, with a little presence of mind, the evil is to be soon surmounted. When the swimmer feels the cramp in his feet or legs, he should forcibly stretch out the limb, and raise the foot up, or rather turn his toes up. This turning up of the toes is an almost certain cure for cramp. If, however, his efforts do not succeed, he should throw himself on his back and float until assistance comes to him. The most important of all is to preserve presence of mind; for, even if the best swimmers give themselves up to fear of cramps, they court the same danger as those who do not know how to swim.

It is seldom that the cramp is so severe as not to allow the swimmer to paddle ashore, or, at any rate, to rest for a while until the pain has passed away or assistance is rendered.

If you find yourself subject to cramp, do not go beyond your depth. Or. if you feel disposed to do so, swim with a friend, for aid in case of necessity is all important. Kick out directly you find the pain coming on, and never mind what momentary agony may accompany the action. Don't hurry, but raise your leg out of the water and turn back your toes as far as you can. If these efforts do not promptly succeed, your companion should seize you by the hair of the head, and push you before him to shore, regardless altogether of any resistance you may offer. Once on shore, rub the limb well with a hard towel or a handful of sand.

It is impossible to say what causes cramp but I think I am not mistaken when I assume that it generally indicates a weak and debilitated state of health.

REMEMBER THESE "POINTERS."

It is hardly necessary to say that salt water is more buoyant than fresh water, but though this is the case, swimming in it is more difficult, by reason of the waves, which are apt to be somewhat wild and contrary now and then. None but very good swimmers should venture far from the shore, though it is true that the waves nearest the shore are the most noisy and turbulent.

Decidedly the most pleasant mode is to swim from a boat a good distance out. The boat, manned by a couple of good swimmers, should be provided with ropes, and fitted at the sides with small ladders, to enable you to get on board without difficulty. Notice the run of the tide, and swim towards land rather than out to sea. Watch the advance of each wave and dive below it rather than attempt to go through or over it. In diving make a good jump wide of the boat, and when tired relieve yourself by floating.

Should a mass of water bear down upon you from behind, wait till it nearly reaches you, and then suddenly dive and swim a little way under water, you will thus avoid being caught on the crest of the wave. It will generally be found that every third, sixth or ninth wave is larger and stronger than the others, and that every such wave is followed by many small waves. In getting to shore, therefore, watch your opportunity, and land as soon as possible after the large wave has broken.

Swimming through the surf may be sometimes necessary, though dangerous. Watch for the small waves, and make your effort at the calmest moment. If a big wave comes, dive; and directly it has passed, swim; then dive again and swim again, and so proceed till your feet are safe on the sands.

Directly you come ashore rub all over with a dry hard towel, and dress immediately after. Never stand about, or you may take a chill that will not be easy to get rid of.

The pupil having overcome the nervousness incident to all first attempts at swimming will soon find that it is much more easy to float than to sink; and this knowledge once acquired, he will have little difficulty in following out any directions given him. If you find that you do not readily take to the water, then a good plan is to float a plank and push it easily before you, so that you can at any time seize it with your bands, as already stated. To support the body on the surface only very slight assistance is necessary, and any swimmer with this knowledge can teach and assist others almost as efficiently as a professor.

A friend may teach nearly as well as a professor; and that, too, without being himself a great or remarkable swimmer. There is no secret in the art of swimming. When once the pupil gets used to the water, he soon takes to plunging, diving, and swimming below it. The learner should be cautioned not to exert himself too much. It is useless to try at the first attempts that which can only come with practice Take it easily, without hurry or bustle, and you will soon learn.

There is no risk swimming in a natatorium, because there are always wideawake eyes to watch, and ready hands to rescue yon at the least sign of danger. Reliance upon the teacher is the first practical lesson with which the learner's mind becomes familiar.

Ernest J. Dick

GENERAL ADVICE-BRIEFLY STATED.

One of the very first requisites for the swimmer who wishes to save his own life or that of another is to know how to float; though, as you know, floating is by no means swimming. Remember that the water will support the body if only you place yourself in the proper position. Many persons are drowned by not attending to a few simple and easily acquired rules.

Exertion in the water is not requisite to preserve the body from sinking; all you have to do is to lie on your back and keep your face above the surface, without attempting to imitate the action of the swimmer. Keep your hands under the water. As the waves pass over you, take advantage of the interval to renew the air in your chest. Keep the lungs as full of air as possible.

Now these rules, fully carried out, will at any rate prevent you from sinking. For you must recollect that keeping the lungs full of air is as good as tying a bladder round your neck or placing corks behind your shoulders. Remember also that the act of raising your hands above the surface, and struggling about, causes you to sink, while, by keeping them below, you can float till assistance arrives. The water in your ears will not hurt

Pursuing Clara

you, though it may cause a humming sound in your head. Nor is it necessary to close the eyes; for the water will not hurt them, beyond, perhaps, a slight tingling sensation. Endeavor by all means to preserve your presence of mind, and do not give way to terror or fright.

So much for your own safety. But in cases where it is necessary to save the life of a comrade or other person in danger of drowning, a different system must be pursued. The first and most important object is to bring your friend ashore. This is sometimes difficult, as drowning persons are very apt to grasp at and cling to you. Shakespeare tells us that drowning men catch at straws. Therefore beware of that catch, as it is very dangerous, both to the drowning man and to the rescuer. When you reach the person in danger, go carefully behind him, without letting him cling to or hold you. Then support his head with your hand under his chin, or your elbow under his arm. But at all hazards bring him ashore as quickly as possible, either above or below the water. Keep your man at arm's length, and prevent him from clinging to you. Then push him before you to shore. A very slight exertion will suffice to keep him from sinking.

In cases where the person is insensible, any means of bringing him quickly ashore may be taken. Raise his head above the surface, and either push him before you, or support him with one arm while you swim with the other, or tread water, or swim on your back; but, in all cases, be prompt. While you display courage, you must beware of rashness.

One great recommendation of swimming is the cleanliness it enforces. Nothing so conduces to health as keeping open the pores of the skin. Swimming does this effectually. Cold water is an excellent tonic.

The first plunge brings a grand reactionary feeling. The body is all in aglow, and a feeling of pleasure immediately follows. If you are cold in the water, and do not feel the glow, you may be sure that you are not in thoroughly good health. and therefore should not bathe—at any rate—not for any length of time.

Directly you feel a chill, leave the water, and give yourself a good rubbing with a rough towel.

Sea-bathing is more stimulating than fresh water swimming; but, whether in fresh or salt water, the exercise is highly commendable.

Don't be content to simply "swim a little."

Beware of weeds and floating grass. Be careful in walking that you do not wound the feet. Look well for signs of quicksand; and do not bathe in a strange surf without an attendant. Do not stay too long in the water, nor allow the hot sun to pour down on your unprotected back or head. Above all, do not imagine that when you have read my book you have done anything more than prepared yourself, somewhat more effectually to receive your first practical lesson.

DR. FRANKLIN'S "KITE" STORY.

Dr. Franklin tells a tale about being drawn through the water by means of a kite. When a boy, he one day, amused himself, he says, by holding the string of his flying kite, and while floating on his back, was drawn by it across a lake. He was so successful that he tried it again and again; and finally expressed himself confident that by such means a man might cross the English Channel! The kite voyage. I take it, was but a dream; for in an American book I have seen it seriously stated that the philosopher COULD NOT SWIM AT ALL.

As a fitting ending to our swimming gossip I will recite the following from Cheever's "Island World in the Pacific":

It was on the same track by which we have thus gained safely our island home that a swimming feat was performed a few years ago by a native woman in peril, which surpasses all other achievements of the kind on record. When about midway between the outmost points of Hawaii and Kahoolawe, or thirty miles from land on either side, a small island vessel, poorly managed and leaky (as they generally are), suddenly shifted cargo in a strong wind, plunged bows under, and went down, there being on board between thirty and forty persons, and a part of them in the cabin

This was just after dinner on Sunday. The natives who happened to be on deck were at once thrown into the waves, with no means of escape but their skill in swimming. A man by the name of Mauae, who had conducted the Sabbath service with the people, now called them around him in the water, and implored help. Then, as a strong current was setting to the North, making it impossible for them to get to Hawaii, whither they were bound, they all made, in different ways, for Maui, and Kahoolawe.

The Captain of the schooner, a foreigner, being unable to swim, was put by his Hawaiian wife on an oar, and they, too, struck out together for the distant shore; but on Monday morning, having survived the first night, the captain died; and in the afternoon of the same day his wife landed on Kahoolawe. A floating hatchway from the wreck gave a chance for life to a strong young man and his brother; but the latter perished before the daylight of Monday, while the elder reached the island in safety by eight or nine o'clock. A feeble boy, without any support, swam the same distance of thirty miles, and reached land safely before any of the others. Mauae and his wife had each secured a covered bucket for a buoy, and three young men kept them company till evening; but all disappeared one after another during the night, either by exhaustion or getting bewildered and turning another way, or by becoming the prey of sharks.

Monday morning the faithful pair were found alone; and the wife's bucket coming to pieces, she swam without anything till the afternoon, when Mauae became too weak to go on. The wife stopped and *loutilomied* him (a kind of shampooing common here), so that he was able to swim again until Kahoolawe was in full view. Soon, however, Mauae grew so weary that he could not even hold to the bucket; and his faithful wife, taking it from him, bade him cling to the long hair of her head, while she still hopefully held on, gradually nearing the shore. Her husband's hands, however, soon slipped from her hair—too weak to keep their hold; and she tried in vain to rouse him to further effort, She endeavored, according to the native expression, to *hoolana kona manao*, 'to make his hope swim,' to inspire him with confidence by pointing to the land, and telling him to pray; but he could only utter a few broken petitions. Putting his arms. therefore, around her own neck, she held them fast with one hand, and still swam vigorously with the other until nearr nightfall, when herself, and her lifeless burden, were within a quarter of a mile from the shore. She had now to contend with the raging surf, and finding the body of her husband, which she had borne so long, stone-dead, she reluctantly cast it off, and shortly after reached land.

But there she was hardly better off than at sea, for long exposure to the brine had so blinded her eyes, that it was sometime before she could see; her strength was too much spent to travel, and the spot on which she landed was barren lava, on the opposite side of the island to any settlement. Food and water she must find or die. Providentially she obtained the latter in the rain that had recently fallen. and that was standing for her in the cups of the rocks. Monday night, Tuesday, Wednesday and Thursday came and went without relief, while she crept on as gradually as she could toward the inhabited part of the island. At last. on Friday morning, when her *manaolana*, her swimming hope, that had held her so long above the waves, was fast sinking with her failing strength, she discovered a water-melon vine in fruit. Eating one, 'her eyes were enlightened,' like Jonathan's, by the honey; soon after she was found by a party of fishermen, by them cared for and conducted to their village, and the next day transported by canoe to Lahaina, whence the foundered schooner had sailed just one week before.

Ernest J. Dick

Appendix B: Extract from *The Romance of Old Annapolis Royal*

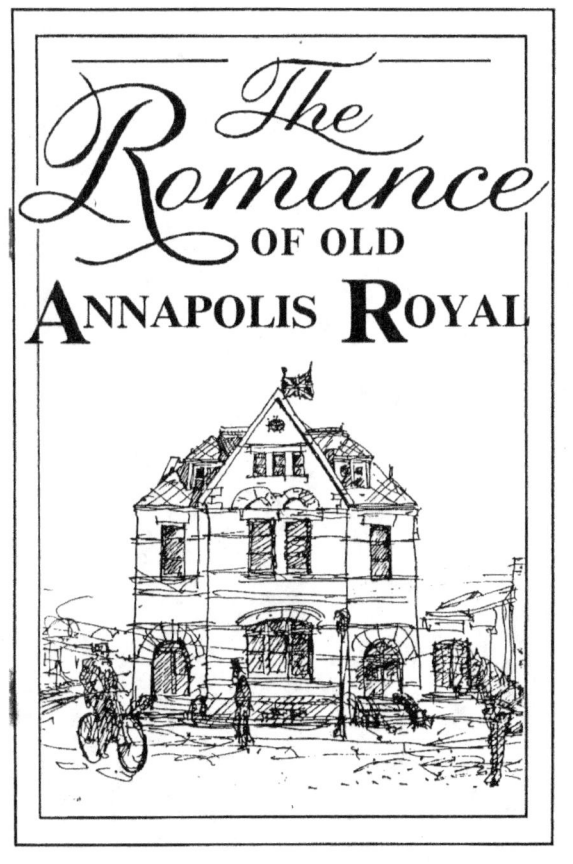

Figure 16: The Old Post Office

Ernest J. Dick

In a section describing the notable houses of Annapolis Royal, the author details the history of the Ritchie House, which is now the Queen Anne Inn.

Another phase in the history of this house was the opening of a private school for boys in 1897....When that closed, again it was left desolate. Then a Mrs. McInnes bought it and thereby hangs a tale—a "Once upon a time" one. When a little girl, Clara Sabeans by name, slim and blond, and most likely in tattered dress, bare feet in summer for her parents were very poor, she used to watch the grand Ritchie house grow and wish she could own it some day—a dream she never lost sight of. The Sabeans then lived in a small old house on Academy Square. Clara helped to eke out a living by selling mushrooms, marsh greens, etc., or by begging. She would say at someone's door that she had a two or three cents to buy a loaf of bread and could she get a few more, or a few cents to go on the Ferry to Granville. She never missed out on anything in town and became intensely interested in watching Mr. W. W. Clarke swim in the Annapolis River. He kindly gave her lessons and under his tutelage she soon became a proficient swimmer. When about seventeen years old, Clara went to Boston on the steamer Hunter, that plied between here and that port. At the beaches there she attracted attention by her stunts and fearlessness in the water, which led up to her being asked to become a performer in the Boston American Swimming Pool. Then a company was formed and she was taken to all the large cities in the U.S.A. as Clara Beckwith, the champion swimmer. Besides this profession with her fine figure, she became a model for sculptors. This was corroborated by Mr. Clarke who, on going into the Washington, D.C., Art Gallery and looking up, exclaimed, "Why, there's Clara!" Occasionally she visited her native town in the summer, and never forgot Mr. Clarke's kindness. Some years passed and then it was known that she had married Mr. McInnes, M.P., Minister of Education for Manitoba, and that he had died, leaving her a wealthy widow.

One day there was quite a flutter in town, for Clara was coming back to fulfil her dream—to buy the Ritchie house. She brought a friend with her, also a lot of baggage. She called the place The Old Orchard House, from the old orchard to the south of it, and began to get ready for tourists. Business boomed in the old town, for she ordered all the best furnishings the merchants could provide—but with promissory payments.

Her house in order, she gave a large reception one evening, and with her friend, graciously received her guests; a large French music box played, while

Pursuing Clara

refreshments were served in the dining room. How did the townspeople react? There were those who scoffed—"Wouldn't think of going," knowing her background. Some went for business reasons, some out of curiosity, while others just to be neighborly—for hadn't she come to live amongst us?

The tourist season was slim that summer, not what she had anticipated, and she had spent considerable money on the place. So, with her resources running low, she suddenly decided to decamp. One evening, she called up the firm of Chas. Dargie & Son, telling them they could have the furniture back as it was just as good as when she bought it. The next morning word quickly got around that she was leaving town and bills not paid! One of her creditors got out a capias, but not soon enough for Clara, for when the policeman arrived with it at the station she was already on the train, waving a calm and smiling good-bye. The merchants afterwards recovered most of their goods.

This was the end of Clara, as far as Annapolis Royal was concerned.

Ernest J. Dick

Appendix C: From 1860s Lambeth to Niagara in the 1900s: Imitation and Innovation amongst Female Natationists

Dave Day

The footnotes for this essay appear in the 'Notes' section at the end of the book.

In the late Victorian period, English amateur sportsmen created regulatory bodies to govern their activities, organisations that proved highly effective in reinforcing the ongoing exclusion of both women and working class participants, especially professionals. Faced by a 'double jeopardy', working class females who had been making a living from displaying their physical talents retreated further from an already limited competitive arena into the world of entertainment. Although working class women generally lacked the necessary freedom of choice, money and time for leisure activities, sports-like amusements had always provided an alternative working environment for a very small number of individuals. During the eighteenth century, the 'European Championess' Elizabeth Stokes recorded forty-five boxing victories and a century later female pedestrianism established an intermittent presence in the Victorian sporting landscape. Ada Anderson worked as an entertainer and theatre manageress before becoming a pedestrienne in 1877, performing a number of long-distance walks including 1,500 miles in 1,000 hours at Leeds in 1878. Her appearances in America stimulated a pedestrian vogue involving over a hundred working class women, many of whom subsequently became professional cyclists. Elsewhere, the formation in 1890 of the Original English Lady Cricketers, recruited from the lower-middle and upper-lower classes, marked the creation of the first professional women's teams in any sport.[27]

The most prominent female professionals of the period were swimmers and, by the end of the century, working class 'naiads' and 'mermaids' were performing before all social classes, in the variety theatre as well as in the swimming pool. Lurline exhibited in a crystal aquarium at the Oxford Music Hall in the 1890s and in October 1889, Ada Webb, 'Champion Lady High Diver of the World and Queen of the Crystal Tank', appeared at the Canterbury Theatre of Varieties where her underwater feats included eating, drinking, smoking, peeling an apple, answering questions, sewing, singing, taking snuff and writing.[28] During 1898, Elise Wallenda remained underwater at the Alhambra for four minutes forty-five and a half seconds. Annie Luker's dives from the Westminster Aquarium roof were widely admired and Marie Finney was presented with a gold medal in recognition of her 'clever and plucky dive from London-bridge' prior to giving an exhibition at the Trocadero Music Hall in 1889. Many natationists also generated careers as swimming teachers, including Fanny Easton and Mrs. Newman.[29]

At Margate in 1884 Professor Frederick Beckwith was teaching in one bath whilst his 'accomplished mermaid of a daughter', Agnes, was teaching women's classes in the other.[30] Frederick involved the whole of his immediate and most of his extended family in aquatic activities between 1850 and 1900 and the Beckwiths became the most renowned swimming family in Britain, while Agnes's appearances in North America created such an impression that her name became synonymous with female swimming excellence. Recognising the commercial potential, American natationists Cora MacFarland and Clara Sabean both claimed a Beckwith lineage, adopted Agnes's performance routines and made successful careers as the 'Champion Lady Swimmer of the World'. All three women had a lifetime's association with swimming, as teachers, competitors and performers, and, in order to uncover commonalities, their stories are presented here as a series of short biographies. Although Bourdieu regarded biographies as illusions, arguing that the straightforward, one-dimensional life story could not exist and that lived lives were chaos, he recognised that individual life-stories can be seen as reflections of social structures and it is by exploring the lives of individuals that scholars can illuminate what Mills called the 'historical push and shove' of society. Merely by existing, each person contributes, however minutely, to the shaping of society and to the course of its history, and Victorian working class females were not merely the passive victims of historical processes but active agents who participated in shaping their world.[31]

Agnes Beckwith

On 24 August 1875, Captain Matthew Webb became the first person to swim the English Channel, immediately establishing himself as a Victorian celebrity. Partly to 'puff up' himself and Agnes, Beckwith took advantage of the interest generated by Webb's success and embarked on a series of endurance swims featuring his daughter, beginning in September 1875 with the fourteen-year-old swimming five miles in the Thames.[32] In 1876, Agnes swam three quarters of a mile in the Tyne and completed over ten miles in the Thames when large crowds watched her using breaststroke, interspersed with displays of trick swimming.[33] In 1878, the now seventeen-year-old swam twenty miles in the Thames and subsequently expressed a desire to attempt the Channel.[34] Although this never materialised, Agnes continued endurance displays and, at the Westminster Royal Aquarium in 1880, she completed a thirty-hour swim, taking all her meals in the water and reading accounts of her swim while still swimming.[35] Agnes subsequently swam for a hundred hours in six days in the Aquarium whale tank and later advertisements described her as the 'Heroine of the 100 hours' swim'.x [36]

While endurance swimming came in for criticism because of the physical excesses involved, racing proved slightly more acceptable and Agnes did compete in a three match series against Laura Saigeman.[37] Ornamental swimming was considered the most appropriate activity for female natationists and aquatic displays utilising swimming baths and glass tanks in aquaria, circuses and music halls provided extensive opportunities for swimming entrepreneurs. Agnes began this type of performance in 1865 and she was appearing regularly at Lambeth Baths by the 1870s. In 1872, Agnes and Willie debuted as Les Enfants Poissons in a plate glass aquarium at the Porcherons Music Hall in Paris and Agnes was a main attraction at the Brighton aquarium.[38] In the 1880s, Agnes had 151 weeks of continuous engagement at the Westminster Aquarium, where she was 'a veritable mermaid', swimming, floating, diving and turning somersaults through hoops, as well as kissing her hand to spectators in 'the most bewitching style'.[39]

In 1882, Agnes married William Taylor, a theatrical agent who was already managing the family, although she kept the Beckwith name for public performances.[40] Agnes exhibited in North America in 1883 and swam in France and Belgium during the 1880s as well as appearing with Hengler's Cirque in Liverpool and Glasgow and with Barnum's 'Greatest Show on Earth' at Madison Square Garden in 1887. An American reporter recalled the excitement in the crowd when Agnes stepped out onto the elevated stage and bowed gracefully before diving into a huge water tank. The 'picturesque aquatic expert' was a comely, blue-eyed, twenty-four-year old English girl with soft hair hung in small curls upon her shoulders. A flowing robe of old gold was wrapped about her from her throat to her feet as she stepped out upon the platform. She tossed off her rubber overshoes and, then flinging aside the robe, she revealed her limbs encased in flesh-coloured tights and a dark-hued jersey drawn snugly about her waist. She dived and waltzed like a swan, turned somersaults, swam under water and climaxed her performance by propelling herself along with graceful undulations of the body while her hands and feet were bound together. During this visit, Agnes gave an interview that established something of a template for her imitators. She said that she had inherited the art from her father, Professor Frederick Beckwith, and that she had learned to be as fond of water as a fish in the Lambeth baths when she was only four years old. She exaggerated somewhat in saying she had been twelve-years-old when she first swam publicly in the Thames but she faithfully recalled her subsequent swims of ten and twenty miles, as well as her continuous swims of thirty hours and one hundred hours in a week.[41]

Agnes returned to England to lead a troupe of female swimmers, whose 'graceful and expert performances' popularised swimming and who pleased everyone by their charming appearance in their pretty costumes,[42] reinforcing the impression that the appeal of female natationists often had as much to do with their physical appearance as their skill. Despite the closure of the Westminster Aquarium and the deaths of her father and brothers during the 1890s, Agnes carried on exhibiting even though her physical charms may have diminished. In February 1903, she had her only child, William Walter Beckwith Taylor, who subsequently performed alongside his mother as 'the youngest swimmer in the World', and Agnes continued to perform and teach at venues as far afield as Hastings, Dover, Aylesbury and Manchester. By 1911, however, she was describing herself as an ex-professional swimmer.[43] In 1916, Agnes married Leopold Solomons and the family name was gradually anglicised to 'Beckwith' Saunders with son William becoming Jack Beckwith Saunders. Agnes, Jack, and his family, sailed for South Africa in 1948, eventually settling in Port Elizabeth. A year later, Agnes was admitted to Nazareth House where she died on 10 July 1951.[44]

The 'Beckwith' name

Even in England, the identity of Beckwith troupe members was often blurred because of the practice of assigning the family name to all and sundry, irrespective of familial relationships. Some, like Agnes's half-sister Lizzie, the professor's youngest daughter, were genuine 'Beckwiths' and Frederick employed Lizzie, or 'Nellie', in his shows from a young age.[45] By 1896, Lizzie had also established herself as a song and dance artist,[46] and she left for America in 1904 to appear in variety. She married a fellow vaudeville artiste later that year but died from pneumonia in Colorado only three months later.[47] Charles Beckwith's daughter Aggie performed at Lambeth Baths in 1899[48] and Willie's wife, Emma, an accomplished ornamental swimmer,[49] appeared regularly with Agnes and her troupe, often as 'Ethel', while non-familial 'Beckwiths' included Dora, May and Mabel.[50]

Following Agnes's performances in 1887, the Beckwith name appeared in American newspaper reports even after her return to England. An Annie Beckwith, described as a 'noted English natator' who had supposedly won a six days' floating competition in London, emerged in Boston in 1888. Annie was described as a charming young woman, not yet nineteen but 'very womanly' in appearance, almost five feet five inches tall, weighing about 140lbs and with an almost perfect figure, a very sweet face and blonde hair. Reports described her as the first cousin of Miss Agnes Beckwith, the natational 'wonder of the world'. A year later, newspapers were reporting a six-day contest in Boston involving eighteen-year-old Alice Beckwith, a cousin of the 'famous English swimmers' Agnes and Willie Beckwith.[51] It is probable that 'Annie' and/or 'Alice' were pseudonyms and that, given their reported ages, they were, in fact, either Clara or Cora 'Beckwith', American born natationists who both had long and successful careers.

Clara 'Beckwith'

Clara Maria Sabean, born in Nova Scotia in October 1870[52], went to Boston around 1887 where she was recruited as a performer in the Boston American Swimming Pool and subsequently promoted as Clara 'Beckwith'.[53] By 1889, her repertoire included tank displays and competitive swimming for wagers, including a six-day event against Valeska Neilson, 'champion of Germany'.[54] During 1890, Clara appeared with a group of young females in the large tank at the Boston Grand Museum and reports in 1891 recorded the 'Diving, Swimming and daring Feats' given by Clara, 'Champion Female Swimmer of the world'.[55] In 1893, she was at Tony Pastor's Theatre as the 'Woman Fish', or 'Water Queen', who lived, ate, walked, played, waltzed, read and acted under the water, while, at the Summer Garden in 1894, she was a 'bewitching, captivating Water Nymph'.[56] During 1895 and 1896, Clara 'disported herself in her swimming tank' day and night at Proctor's Theatre and at Proctor's Pleasure Palace in New York, alongside vaudeville, minstrelsy, acrobats and the 'original comedy elephants'.[57]

Her show was described in detail in 1893. After 'the champion lady swimmer of the world,' had been introduced, the 'trim figure in Mephistophelian red tripped up the stepladder to the top of the tank and sank into the water'. When submerged she turned somersaults and lay at the bottom as if sleeping. She played with a 60lb dumbbell underwater, ate a banana, drank a bottle of milk and then chalked her name on a slate, which she pressed against the sides for the audience to read. She sewed two pieces of cloth together, taking about twenty-five stitches without surfacing, and then walked along the bottom on her hands. Her exhibition of a person drowning was so realistic that many spectators 'experienced cold chills' at her screams. She sank to the bottom like a drowning body and lay face downward, after which she rose to the surface and floated like a dead body before turning over and becoming again 'the modern mermaid'.[58]

Clara said she was five feet four inches tall although 1893 reports described her as so upright that she looked taller and younger than her given age of twenty-five, with dark brown hair, grey and clear eyes and a fine complexion. She was a well-formed, strong athlete who seemed lighter than her average weight of 150lbs and it was difficult to believe that she could lift 200lbs dead weight. In her swimming suit Clara showed the almost perfect development which her training had produced.[59]

Clara married Stanley McInnis in June 1898, which probably accounts for the fact that there are few references to her in subsequent years, and when he died in 1907, he left Clara a wealthy widow.[60] In a rare display of honesty regarding her origins, Clara described herself at her marriage as Clara Marie Sabean born in October 1870 in Nova Scotia but in the 1901 census, she declared she was twenty-seven having been born in 1873 in England and arriving in Canada in 1887. When she married Clement Miller in 1908, Clara called herself Clara M. Beckwith McInnis, born circa 1872 in England. In 1910, Clara claimed she was thirty-six, that she had been born in England and that she had arrived in America in 1890.[61] This heritage had been crafted over some years and was made explicit in her 1893 autobiography, which claimed she had been born in Lambeth in October 1867. Her father, William Manning Beckwith, had been champion swimmer of England for ten consecutive years and, after he relinquished the title, it had passed to her brother Willie who had successfully defended it ever since. Her younger brother, Charles, was an excellent swimmer while Agnes, her sister, was an expert of the highest order. Clara's first public appearance had been when she was thirteen-years-old, after which her father had predicted that eventually she would be recognised as the 'Champion Lady Swimmer of the World.' With his encouragement, she had issued challenges to English female professionals but, after two years of no acceptances, the title of Champion had been conceded to her, following which Clara said 'farewell to Lambeth and its fond associations', and travelled to Boston in 1882.[62]

In a widely syndicated newspaper interview in July 1893, Clara reinforced her Beckwith origins in the public imagination. She had been born in Lambeth, England, and was a member of the famous Beckwith family of swimmers. When asked how she had learnt to swim she said 'Oh, it's born in me, I guess...All my family swim...Father and Willie and Charley and my sister Agnes.' Clara went on:

> We lived near the beach, and I was always running down to the water, but I had never been taught to swim and I didn't know how. One day, when I was twelve years old and I was paddling around a big wave came along and carried me off my feet. I caught my breath and struck right out with a breast-stroke and, because I did not know how to turn around, I kept on swimming until someone saw me and came to my rescue in a boat. [63]

In her autobiography, Clara observed that during her professional career the press had called her 'The Modern Mermaid,' 'Neptune's favored daughter,' 'The water Nymph' and 'Naiad of the deep.' She was only grateful that 'her nature was not susceptible to flattery' although she was proud of being recognised as the 'Champion lady Swimmer of the World', an achievement acquired by perseverance, hard work and determination. It was her earnest wish, apparently, in reciting her 'life in the water' to avoid all semblance of egotism and self-laudation.[64] It has to be said that this went somewhat against the normal practices of professional natationists, including Clara, and Cora 'Beckwith', another self-proclaimed 'Champion Lady swimmer of the World', proved to be far less reticent.

Cora 'Beckwith'

Cora McFarland was born in 1869 in Maine and, within twenty years, she had become a professional natationist performing as Cora 'Beckwith' in the tank at the Grand Dime Museum. The bill included future husband Charles M. Ernest who performed a 'burnt cork comedy' routine, involving stereotypical caricatures of a black person.[65] Cora, the 'champion lady swimmer of the world', performed at the Retail Clerks' Picnic at Wildwood in 1893, lived in a tank for seven days at the Casino in 1894[66] and was the main feature at the Circus Royal and Venetian Water Carnival in San Francisco in 1895 where she introduced 'many strange tricks of her own invention'. Apparently, she had been 'lionized by society' which might have spoiled her but for the 'brave little lady's level head'.[67]

Theatre impresario Jake Rosenthal, who managed both Al Jolson and Houdini, became Cora's manager in 1895 and married her after she divorced Charles.[68] Jake promoted Cora to managers of seaside and summer resorts, summer gardens, outdoor entertainments and vaudeville houses as an exponent of natatorial feats. She floated for thirty days at the Boston Zoo and her troupe of young swimmers could be seen in a tank in the lecture hall at Austin and Stone's Museum during 1898.[69] In 1899, Cora could be seen at Fairmount Park in June, performing and giving swimming lessons to women,[70] and again at Cedar Point in July where, among other feats, she demonstrated the English sidestroke, her own invention—the Beckwith backward sweep, the dead float, the double overhead stroke and waltzing.[71]

At the Pan-American Exposition at Buffalo in 1901, Cora's Natatorium, one of the few concessions that made money, featured the 'World's Greatest swimmer, Champion Trick and fancy swimmer of All Europe and Pan American'. For between fifteen and twenty-five cents she could be seen 'living, sleeping, and eating' in a tank filled with four feet of water for up to nine hours every day.[72] Cora had 'sleek hair as black as jet, with flesh as soft and pliable as that of a baby', her body shape had been moulded by its long caress with water and, while 'a trifle stout', it was 'in its full strength of a superb womanhood'. Her hands and feet were 'prettily turned' and her shoulders and torso were as finely developed as 'those of the most expert boxer'.[73]

Just as Agnes spent her summers at English seaside resorts, Cora established her own season touring fairs, carnivals and festivals, although she had to take the paraphernalia of her performances with her since there were few swimming baths.[74] Between 1902 and 1904, Cora appeared at McBeth's Park, at the Logan Free Carnival and as the 'human fish' at a fair and carnival in Saratoga. At the 'Redmen's Pow-wow and carnival' in 1904 she illustrated the strokes used by different nations, strokes of her own design and a 'mystifying' method of floating in which not a muscle moved.[75] Like Agnes, Cora spent the winters touring indoor facilities with a troupe of female swimmers. At the Clark Street Dime Museum in 1901, Cora's women swimmers were a chief attraction, and her 'Neptune's Daughters', featuring four young women performing trick and fancy diving at the Strand in 1917, was considered one of the 'prettiest' aquatic entertainments in vaudeville.[76]

When Cora died in 1924 her death certificate referred to her as Cora 'Beckwith' Rosenthal.[77] During her lifetime, reports had consistently established connections between her and the genuine Beckwith family both in terms of lineage and of natational performances. Performing at the Casino in 1894 she was referred to as Cora Beckwith of England, in 1895 she was described as having delighted the 'British public for years' and in 1899 she was advertised as a British subject straight from the Royal Aquarium in London.[78] Cora contributed to the deception, describing how she had been born into an English family of noted swimmers and she had taken to the water as a two-year-old following the example of her father, a famous swimming professional and 'keeper of the Royal Aquarium at Westminster'. According to Cora she had started exhibiting at five, swum the Thames at eleven, jumped from London bridge when she was thirteen and floated ten hours a day for forty consecutive days.[79]

'Puffing up' Cora: The Niagara rapids 'ballyhoo'

A reporter observed in 1899 that the 'ballyhoo' surrounding Cora's shows was one of its major drawing cards[80] and Cora's most outrageous claim was that she had swum the English Channel, aged fifteen or sixteen, either alongside Webb or having been the only female or indeed person to have ever done so.[81] Her aquatic 'feats' had made her 'the most talked of woman in the world' and Cora extended this 'ballyhoo' by announcing regularly that she would swim the Niagara rapids. The idea first emerged in 1895, although it was really in 1901, at the time of her engagement at the Pan-American Exposition, that Cora revived the prospect of swimming the rapids.[82] When asked if she was not worried that she would meet the fate of Webb, who had drowned there, she said:

> 'I have no fear of the rapids. I have visited them three times recently and thrown sticks and stones into the water and have failed to find anything awful about the rapids. I shall visit them every Sunday from now until the date of my performance to study the currents and get the proper bearings. I expect to get through the rapids without any difficulty by floating on my back'.[83]

In another interview, Cora said she had seen Webb swim to his death after she had told him 'he was foolish to keep so near the Canadian shore'. There was only one thing in the gorge which frightened her, 'a razorlike lip of a ledge of bright red granite' although she had found a way to avoid it. According to

Cora, she was able to float better than Webb and, since she could also stay underwater for four minutes, her plan was to float down the rapids making no movements except those necessary to keep her nose and mouth above water.[84]

The announcement certainly generated the requisite interest. Cora was invited to Richmond to give an exhibition and George Farrell who was preparing to cross the Falls on a bicycle delayed his attempt because Cora wanted him to do a double act with her.[85] Unsurprisingly, this attempt did not materialise although the 'ballyhoo' was repeated in 1902, 1903, and again in 1904 when Cora 'upped the stakes' by declaring that she would swim the rapids 'or perish'.[86] The *Niagara Falls Gazette* was sceptical about her 'fairy tales' proposing a swim through the rapids. Cora had previously attracted notoriety by saying she intended to swim the rapids and now she was 'handing out a few dope stories' again. Although a good swimmer, Cora 'never swam the whirlpool rapids and does not intend to'. In 1912, Cora again announced a Niagara attempt and, despite the lack of concrete evidence, it was reported in 1917 that 'some years ago' she had swum 'a dangerous passage at Niagara Falls, one which was never before accomplished by a lady swimmer'.[87]

Some reflections
The close relationship between entertainment and sport highlighted here by the biographies of these 'Beckwith' natationists was not unique to the activ-

ity, or to the period, since professional athletes, aware of the transitory nature of their earning potential, have always explored every potential outlet in order to capitalise on their reputation. While women earning their living by swimming-related activities were few in number, their public performances were still receiving considerable publicity around the turn of the twentieth century, at which point Agnes remained the most prominent female swimmer in the public imagination, both at home and abroad. Although she was never able to convert this social capital into personal financial capital, her appearances in America in 1883 and 1887 clearly stimulated imitation and, by adopting the name and appropriating the methods and techniques of the original, both Clara and Cora transported her skills across America. There is some evidence that these two women were aware of each other's existence. In 1889, Clara concluded that Cora had decided not to respond to her challenge for a six days' swimming match so she offered her rival for the title of champion woman swimmer another chance to prove her superiority.[88] The fact that Cora did not respond is almost certainly a sign of good judgement since the swimming careers of the two women would suggest that Clara was more used to racing in this kind of event and would have started with an advantage. This has echoes of the reluctance of Frederick and Agnes to engage in head-to-head races with opponents who were patently faster over short distances, since defeat would dent Agnes's status as the world's leading female natationist.

Much more work needs to be done to uncover what Bale calls the 'layers of truth'[89] regarding these natatorial careers but, even at this stage, these women's lives raise some interesting points, not least about the use of physical display as entertainment, making it a distinct entity and separate from sport. Other questions arise concerning the methods used by professionals to 'puff up', the content of natatorial displays, the influence of males as managers and husbands, and the use of emerging technology.

Clara, who generally appeared on stages rather than at fairs, performed on one occasion in a tank ten feet long, four feet wide and eight feet deep containing salted water and heated to 92° while, at the Washington Lyceum, she had a tank fifty feet long.[90] Because her summer was predominantly spent in rural fairs, the organisation and equipment required by Cora was substantial and her entourage was extensive. Charles Snyder of Charleston had been her showman in 1897 but, by 1912, her roster included Jake Rosenthal, manager and lecturer, George Hobbs, lecturer and press agent, C.H. Jennings, Mrs. G.M. Hodge, ticket seller, Clarence Mitchell, in charge of natatorium, and Will Clemens, Jr., in charge of the canvas. At the Circus Royal and Venetian Water Carnival in San Francisco in 1895, the circus ring was covered with a 'tremendous rubber', filled with four feet of water, and lithographs of her performances were available later that year.[91] In 1899, the spectacular night exhibition she gave in Fairmount Park was lit by searchlights while the front of her 'Blue Grotto' on West Midway later that year, which resembled the entrance to a huge stone cave, was surrounded by electric lights. When Cora appeared at the Logan Free Carnival in 1903 an excavation fifty feet by twenty feet was made for the exhibition and, in 1904, she exhibited in a portable tank fifty feet long. In 1906, Cora utilised a new outfit for the season, including a canvas, a ten-foot by fifty-foot tank and a special coach and baggage car. In 1907, she used another new tent and a tank holding 40,000 gallons of water, heated by the boiler that powered the merry-go-round, while at the 1908 Marion Inter-State Fair Cora performed in an artificial lake.[92]

Part of this emerging technology was the improvement in communications and this narrative highlights the international reach of the Beckwith 'brand'. By adopting the name and appropriating the methods and techniques of Agnes, both Clara and Cora perpetuated the 'Beckwith' legend and, in a world that was less globalised than it is today, it was comparatively easy for them to duplicate routines without fear of any consequences, especially since the professor and his sons died during the 1890s. Although Lizzie was performing in America at the same time as Cora was touring the rural fairs, no one was ever really in a position to dispute either the appropriation of the Beckwith name or the feats that had proved popular with the paying public. In fact, even if the real Beckwiths had been aware of these initiatives, they may have remained sanguine about anything that kept the name 'Beckwith' in the public arena. If imitation really is the sincerest form of flattery then the original Beckwiths may have been perfectly satisfied with the situation.

Ernest J. Dick

Appendix D: Timeline

*Some entries of dubious authenticity appear with asterisks, as *Clara Beckwith*.*

1818 *The Art of Swimming* encourages parents to teach their sons to swim and included a letter of endorsement by Benjamin Franklin.
1857 Frederick Edward Beckwith, father of Agnes Charlie and Willie Beckwith publishes *The Whole Art of Swimming*.
1863 Agnes Beckwith is born in Lambeth, England.
1864 Wilbert W. 'Bert' Clarke is born in Hantsport, Nova Scotia.
1865 8 October: Stanley McInnis is born in Saint John, New Brunswick.
1867 1 November: Clement G. Miller is born in Boston, Massachusetts.
1869 The Windsor and Annapolis Railway terminates at Annapolis Royal, affording a connection via steam ships to the rest of the world.
1870 22 or 28 October: Clara Maria/Marie Sabean is born in Paradise/Wilmot, Nova Scotia; daughter of Manning Sabean, farmer, (born in Port Lorne) and Jane Wade (born in Granville), married 22 August, 1868 in Parker's Cove.
1871 20 December: Theodore Tebbetts is born in Lynn, Massachusetts.
1874 15 November: Caroline A. Hardwicke is born in Annapolis Royal.
1875 William Ritchie house is built on upper St. George Street in Annapolis Royal, eventually becoming 'The Old Orchard House' in 1909.

24 August: Matthew Webb becomes the first person to swim the English Channel.

1 September: Agnes Beckwith accomplishes a long distance swim in the Thames River from London Bridge to Greenwich, a distance of about 6 miles.

1876 Charlotte Perkins is born in Annapolis Royal.

1877 Eliza Bennett swims across the Hudson River in New York City in August.

1880 In May, Agnes Beckwith treads water for 30 hours in the whale tank of the Royal Aquarium of Westminster to equal time by Matthew Webb. She takes her meals in water, reading accounts of her progress while in the water.

In September, Agnes Beckwith completed 100 hours in the water in six days.

1881 The census reports that Manning Sabean, Baptist and farm labourer, 39; and Jane, Church of England, 32, are living in Granville Ferry with son Fredrick, 11, daughter Clara, 10, son Minard, 8, daughter Nancy, 4, and son Bud, 2 (with 3 oldest children listed as attending school).

1882 In September a rink is being built in Annapolis Royal to be used for agricultural exhibitions, dances, skating, roller-skating, and walking races.

1883 June 5: Willie and Agnes Beckwith arrive on the *City of Berlin* in New York City. Agnes fails in attempt to swim the 20 mile distance from Sandy Hook, New Jersey to Rockaway Pier, New York – swimming 15 miles "before a storm forced her out of the water, against her will".

9 August: Willie and Agnes Beckwith visit Toronto.

1886 Family of Jane Sabean (also spelled Sabin) and three children immigrated to US.

December Agnes Beckwith appears with P. T. Barnum at Madison Square Garden.

1887 Clara immigrates to Canada from England, according to 1901 census.

Annette Kellerman born in Australia.

20 March: Willie and Agnes Beckwith appear with P. T. Barnum at Madison Square Garden.

1888 13 November *Boston Herald*: "The tanks used are immense affairs, each holding 20,000 gallons of water, which is kept at a constant temperature by means of coils of steam pipes. In the water float the young ladies who are contesting for a $1,000 purse. The contestant remaining in the water the longest during the week is to receive the grand prize. Thousands visited the Grand Dime during the afternoon and evening to witness this odd exhibition."

18 November *Boston Herald:* 'Girls Still Floating' "The floating contest did not end yesterday at the Grand Museum as both ladies had 11;15 pm, Saturday completed 65 hours. The contest will go on until one or the other succumbs to exhaustion. Miss Beckwith has lost of over 12 pounds of flesh since she began this peculiar contest. Miss Adams has also become less plump than she was when she entered the water a week ago. Admiring auditors keep the huge basins in which they float well supplied with bouquets of flowers."

Boston Herald: "Miss Beckwith is a charming young lady, not yet 19 years of age, though she is very womanly in appearance. She has an almost perfect figure, a very sweet face, and blonde hair. She stands almost five foot five inches high, weighs 140 pounds. She is first cousin of Miss Agnes Beckwith, noted natator of the world, who with her brother are wonders of the world, in their art. Miss Annie Beckwith, who has not yet a record as long as her most fortunate cousin, but her recent performance stamp her as hardly second to any female natator in

Europe. She recently won a six-days floating contest in one of the large halls of London, defeating many good natators of her sex."

25 November *Boston Herald:* 'Lady Swimming Match for $1,000 a Side' "The great international six-day swimming match for the above amount will commence at noon tomorrow, MONDAY, in the new natatorium, occupying the central division of the Grand Museum between Miss Amy Rogers, recognized lady swimmer champion of America and Miss Annie Beckwith, Famous English Lady Natator. Both ladies will use the peculiar English side stroke, made famous by the late Captain Webb. There will be 100 laps to the mile, each lady will have their own scorer and each lap and mile will be recorded on a score board. Although this will be a most sensational contest no advance will be made in prices as usual 10 cents. The race will start promptly at 12 tomorrow with nurses, judge, referee and physicians on the platform."

1889 27 January *Boston Globe* and *Boston Herald*: Reports of "novel entertainment" at 'Boston Grand Museum' for a purse of $1,000 with Clara Beckwith swimming against Annie Fern: "As a swimmer Miss Fern has few equals and she confidently expects to defeat Miss Beckwith. The young women were matched through the efforts of Mr. Fred Kyle, well known manager of the late captain Matthew Webb."

29 January *Boston Herald*: "Immense crowds at Grand Museum yesterday for the beginning of six-day race for $1,000 between Clara Beckwith and Annie Fern. Miss Beckwith's superb uniform was attired in a silken jersey and leotard of a delicate pink hue. Miss Fern, a delicate looking young lady wore a red jersey and black leotards. Both looked confident."

30 January *Buffalo Express*: "A novel competition, a six-day swimming match between two young women is underway, or under water, in Boston. The contestants are Miss Clara Beckwith of England and Miss Annie Fern. The match is for $1,000 a side. So far Miss Beckwith has demonstrated that she is superior to any other lady swimmer in America."

2 February *Boston Herald*: "BECKWITH VS DYAS - Miss Clara Beckwith, handsomest lady in America and champion swimmer of the world and Miss Maggie Dyas, a beautiful little natator in a six-day swim for $1,000. Race starts soon after 12:00 pm today – at Grand Museum."

Beginning of a "SIX DAYS SWIM" between Clara Beckwith and Annie Fern announced in the *Boston Herald* and *New York Clipper*.

3 February *Boston Herald*: "Miss Clara Beckwith will give exhibitions in the Natatorium of the Grand Museum, corner Washington and Dover Streets, for one week, commencing tomorrow at noon. Miss Clara Beckwith is the handsomest lady in America. She is the champion natator of the world. The management are ready to match her for a one- or six-day swim for one to five thousand dollars. Miss Clara Beckwith did accomplish last week, at this place, a feat that has never been attempted by any lady since old mythical Mother Eve was supposed to start the race. The entire troop of lady natators will take headers in the bath at noon. Miss Cora Rogers, Miss Annie Fern, Miss Maggie Dyas, Miss Mamie Dassitt and others. The water feats will be double sommersaults, head walking, twisting, doubling, folding, the water wheel, the amature

bather, the rocking horse, the angel's prayer, a corpse in the water, rescue from drowning, Adam and Eve, The Greek Goddess, and some fifty other difficult aquatic feats."

4 February *Boston Globe*: "Twisting Somersaults by the beautiful Clara Beckwith. Head Walking by the charming Miss Cora Rogers. One hundred dazzling and dangerous water acts by Miss Maggie Dassit, Miss Annie Fern, and Miss Georgie Faris. Soon after noon today the entire troop of Lady Natators will take headers in the bath at the Grand Museum."

7 February *Buffalo Courier*: "A six-day female swimming match for the champion ship of America between Miss Clara Beckwith and a combination of ladies including Miss Fern, Miss Rogers, and Miss Dyas came to a close in Boston on Saturday night. Miss Beckwith won with a score of 35 miles, 39 laps against 28 miles, 21 laps scored by the combination, which Miss Dyas represented for the last 4 days of the race."

1 March *Boston Herald*: "DROWNING GIRL – the thrilling act presented daily by the lady natators in the Natatorium of the Grand Museum"

2 March *The Progress*: "Six-day swimming match between Clara Beckwith from England and Annie Fern of Boston, commencing on 4th, purse of $1,000 in Boston."

3 March *Boston Globe*: "In the Natatorium during the week will be seen many interesting exhibitions by the expert young lady swimmers, led by Miss Beckwith. The young ladies are seen in the huge bath almost continuously from noon until 9:00 pm."

Pursuing Clara

Boston Globe: "WATER QUEENS - These water queens give exhibitions in Swimming, Floating, Diving, Life Saving, Dead Body Floating, Head Walking, the Moving Raft, the Moving Steamboat and about 50 more. The ladies enter the water daily at 12 noon."

10 March *Boston Globe*: "BIG SWIM - Miss May Morrison from South Boston has the nerve and produced the money for a six-day swim with the unconquered and invincible Clara, the Great MISS BECKWITH. Miss Clara Beckwith is 'somebody' whose name is now a household word. The match is for One Thousand Dollars. The race will be started tomorrow at 12:30 punctually, and at the same hour every day during the week. The judge and referee are from the *Herald* and the *Globe*. There are 42 laps to the mile. The ladies swim all afternoon and all evening. This, the greatest swimming match ever attempted will take place in the Natatorium of the Grand Museum. The ladies will be attired in the regulation Leotard Swimming Costume."

12 March *Boston Herald*: "Miss Clara Beckwith swimming against May Sonson, a very pretty Swedish natator. $1,000 purse put by Museum management and partially by backers of both girls. At 9 o'clock, the close of the match for the day Miss Beckwith had seven miles, 16 laps to her credit to 6 miles 38 laps, or 2 laps short of 7 miles to the credit of Miss Sonson. AT 12.30 the ladies will enter the water for the second day's swim and remain in the water until 9:00 tonight – unless one gives in before that time."

13 March *Boston Globe*: "MET HER MATCH - Sonson is waiting for the last three days of the Race. Clara Beckwith and Mary Sonson, the contestants in the six-days' swimming match at the Grand Museum, are making good records. The natatorium was surrounded yesterday by a large crowd. Miss Beckwith worked steadily in the hope of securing a good lead on her Swedish rival, but only succeeded in gaining a few laps. Miss Sonson is not exerting herself, but her friends say that during the last three days she will force her opponent so hard that if the latter should win it will be only by a short distance. When they left the tank last night the score was: Beckwith, 15 miles 25 laps Sonson, 14 miles 18 laps."

31 March *Boston Herald*: "MISS CLARA BECKWITH – the living goddess of all that is graceful, beautiful and inviting, and the champion swimmer of the world, will be in the Nataorium of the Grand Museum during the coming week".

30 April *Boston Herald*: "The drowning dude act at the Grand Museum and Natatorium, corner of Washington and Dover is one of the most amusing and surprising acts yet presented by the female swimmers and Miss Clara Beckwith, yesterday delighted hundreds at this exhibition with her powers as a character actress as well as a swimmer."

May *Boston Herald, Boston Globe*: "Six-day swimming match beginning tomorrow. The contestants will be Miss Clara Beckwith, champion female swimmer of America and six of the best female natators of the East. The sextet will combine to beat Miss Beckwith, one lady swimmer against her each day."

3 July *Boston Globe*: "Engagement Extraordinary on July 4th for Crescent Beach at Ocean Pier. Cora Beckwith (the original), the world famous swimmer, Miss Beckwith must not be confused with any imitators who have used the name. She is the only original Miss Beckwith. She will be assisted by Prof Naifled, the well-known natator. Among the various feats performed by Miss Beckwith are the straight dive, 90 somersaults under water, the tugboat, water waltz, hand walking, double floating, feet to feet, Life Saving, double somersault, double back somersault."

4 July *Boston Globe*, *Boston Herald*: Ads of Cora Beckwith performing in swimming exhibitions at 'Pilling's World Museum'.

Boston Herald: "Miss Clara Beckwith, champion lady swimmer of the world, is not in Boston, and will not appear at any swimming exhibition in America or England until she commences her fall engagement early in August at the Grand Natatorium, early in the corner of Dover and Washington Streets under the management of G. E. Lothrup. Anyone using the name Beckwith as a swimmer to appear at any summer resort are doing so to deceive the public. Clara will be spending the summer at a cottage at Ocean Grove, New Jersey, with her mother and sister. She will not appear in public till the opening of the Grand Museum and Natorium early in August. To the public: I have signed a contract not to exhibit at any place other than

Ernest J. Dick

the Grand Museum and Natatorium, corner Washington and Dover Street."

21 July *Boston Herald*: "BECKWITH WILL SWIM ANY LADY - To the editor: From recent announcements that I have read in the Boston papers, I feel called upon in justice to the public and myself to state that I have not appeared in public since June 17th and will not appear again until late August. I again repeat my challenge to swim against any lady in the world for $500 or $1000 a side – Clara Beckwith, champion lady swimmer of the world, from Brighton Beach Hotel, Coney Island."

28 July *Boston Globe*: Clara Beckwith reported swimming at Brighton beach, Coney Island, not appearing at 'Grand Museum' until its opening in August.

Boston Herald: "CORA BECKWITH AT PILLING'S WORLD MUSEUM: Manager Pilling has given an order to a Boston photographer for 100,000 photos of Cora Beckwith for free distribution."

8-11 August *Boston Herald*: "After 10 weeks leisure at Coney Island, the great and only champion natator of the world, and the most graceful little athlete of the world who has ever achieved gladiatorial honours, the great and invincible CLARA BECKWITH will appear in her marvellous and daring Aquatic acts."

10 August *New York Clipper*: "Clara Beckwith has returned from Saratoga and will appear in the tank scene in 'A Dark Secret' soon to be produced at the Providence Museum."

11 August *Boston Herald*: "A new natatorium has been built, measuring 80 feet in length... north and south sides

have been transformed into a tropical garden, with cactus plants, large macaws, and many singing birds."

13 August *Boston Herald*: "The Grand Museum has opened with big boom. Manager Lothrop presents a fine bill....Clara Beckwith the pretty and shapely champion swimmer is a great favourite and her performances in the large tank of water are always attractive to large crowds. The young English and Swedish girls will be the leading attractions at this house for some time to come."

17 August *Boston Herald*: "RETURN OF LADY CHAMPION SWIMMER - Clara Beckwith, after an absence in New York of 10 weeks. MONSTER NEW BATH, 100 feet long, containing 100 gallons of water, Monster Troupe of English Swimmers."

August *Boston Herald*: Clara Beckwith and the English and Swedish girls were reported giving exhibitions in the huge tank at the 'Grand Museum', surrounded all day by crowds of admirers. Clara Beckwith, "Champion of the World", was promised as being at every performance.

2 September *Boston Daily Globe*: "MISS CLARA BECKWITH - Handsomest lady in America and champion lady swimmer open to a six-day swimming match with any man in America or any women in the world from $1,000 to $3,000 at Boston Museum."

4 September *Boston Herald*: "This week at the Grand Museum a monster troupe of Beautiful Lady Natators dressed in leotards enter the giant bath at 12:30 and remain there until 9:00pm – Miss Clara Beckwith, Champion Lady swimmer of the world appearing day and evening in daring feats."

Ernest J. Dick

8 September *Boston Daily Globe*: "MISS CLARA BECKWITH MAKES A BUSINESS-LIKE PROPOSITION - Clara Beckwith, the well-known professional swimmer, called at the *Globe* office yesterday and left the following challenge, together with a forfeit: To the Sporting Editor of the *Globe*: A women has taken my name and has been advertised as the champion swimmer of the world. I hereby challenge her to a six-day swimming match for $2,000 a side, and to show that I mean business 1 deposit $500 in your hands and $500 in the hands of the sporting editor of the *Herald*. As this woman is in Boston, this challenge will remain open for two days. (Signed) Clara Beckwith, Champion swimmer of the world, Boston Grand Museum corner of Dover and Washington Streets"

Boston Daily Globe: "At the 'Grand Museum' you see the great and only Champion Swimmer of the World, Miss Clara Beckwith and a Troupe of Beautiful Lady Swimmers, divers, plungers, floaters, hand-walkers, feet-walkers, hand-walkers. Double summer-saults, Sixteen Hand-springs, The Pyramids, the Duck Hunt and Hundreds of dangerous and daring water acts."

11 September *Boston Herald*: "THE RIVAL SWIMMERS – Miss Clara Beckwith, the swimmer, is satisfied that Miss Cora Beckwith has concluded to pay no attention to her recent challenge for a six-days swimming match. Miss Clara now offers her rival for the title of champion woman swimmer another chance to prove her superiority. She will swim Miss Cora Beckwith a six-day race and will let the latter name the hours for swimming, and she is now willing to place $2,000 against Cora's $1,000 that

she will win the race. Furthermore Miss Clara will give her opponent five hours start but reserves the right to name the time and place of holding the match. A cheque for $500 has been left with the Herald as an earnest of good faith."

25-26 September *Boston Globe, Poughkeepsie Daily Eagle*: "Valeska Nelson puts up $500 for race with Clara Beckwith. Valeska Neilson, the Champion swimmer of Germany, wants to swim Clara Beckwiith, Champion swimmer of America. Nelson called the *Globe* office yesterday and stated that she would like to meet Beckwith in a six-day race, and expressed herself as confident of winning. I can put up $1,000 she said. Furthermore, I agree to swim her in the natatorium where she has been doing all of her swimming."

27-28 September *Boston Globe, New York Times*: "WILL SWIM FOR SIX DAYS - Articles of Agreement between Misses Beckwith and Neilson. The six-day swimming match for $1,000 a side and a purse of $1,000 additional will begin Monday. Miss Neilson did not wish to have the race for three weeks to come, but owing to the liberal purse offered by Manager Lothrop, she consented to have it begin Monday next. Articles of agreement were arranged at the Sherman House yesterday afternoon."

October *Boston Herald, Buffalo Courier, Wheeling Register, Duluth Evening Herald, St. Louis Dispatch, New York Clipper, Daily Illinois State Journal* and others: Reports on Clara Beckwith leading the six-day race at the 'Grand Museum'.

Ernest J. Dick

1 October *Boston Globe*: "BIG SWIM starts at 12:30 with Neilson and Beckwith starting at 12:30, orchestra begins at 12:00 – 'Grand Museum'".

13 October *Boston Herald*: "Clara Beckwith giving exhibitions at 'Grand Museum'. Manager Lothrop of the Grand Dime Museum offers to back either Miss Dyas or Miss Beckwith against Swimmer Leavitt for $1,000. Miss Beckwith will give Leavitt 10 miles start in a six-day race and Miss Dyas will give him 5 miles on a race of the same length."

1890 25 May *Boston Globe*, *Boston Herald*: "FOR A PURSE OF $250 - Clara Beckwith and Katie Anderson to swim at the Howard. William Harris has offered Misses Clara Beckwith and Katie Anderson the use of the large tank in 'A Dark Secret' now playing at the Howard Atheneum for their swimming contest for the quarter-mile championship. The ladies will swim a quarter mile at each of the nine performances during the week, beginning tomorrow and on Saturday evening the contestant winning the greater number of times will be presented with a purse of $250. The audience will act as judges at each performance."

Boston Herald: "The girls, Clara Beckwith and Katie Anderson, will be dressed in neat and attractive suits displaying their well-formed figures to good advantage will swim as above."

27 May *Boston Daily Advertiser*: "'A Dark Secret' continues on the boards at the Howard Atheneum this week. This play is very popular with Boston Theatre goers and is very ably presented by the present company. The Henley regatta scene is very handsome and the result of the

boat race attracts as much enthusiasm as though it was a reality. A novel feature of the Henley scene was a swimming race for $250 between Miss Clara Beckwith and Miss Katie Anderson. The ladies are to swim one quarter of a mile each evening of the week, and the one winning the most events Saturday is to be named the final winner. Miss Beckwith won the event last evening in 6 minutes 22 seconds, gaining one lap on her opponent. This race was much enjoyed in the upper part of the house, but the swimmers were invisible from the orchestra floor."

28 May *Boston Globe*: "Monday night Beckwith finished one lap ahead of her competitor but last night Anderson clearly outswam her competitor, finishing the second quarter-mile three seconds ahead with Anderson 6 mn 40seconds to Beckwith at 6 mn 43 seconds."

27 July *Boston Herald*: "CLARA BECKWITH is on deck for the season at the Boston Grand Museum, after seven months in Europe and five weeks leisure at Coney Island to undergo the necessary training. The Great and Only Champion Natator of the World, and the most beautiful and graceful athlete who has ever achieved gladiatorial honours the, great and invincible MISS CLARA BECKWITH Will appear in her marvellous and daring aquatic acts."

29 July *Boston Herald*: "GRAND MUSEUM OPENING – the museum has been completely renovated and presents a very handsome appearance. The attractions for the opening were excellent. First, Miss Clara Beckwith, champion lady swimmer of the world, with her startling aquatic feats and surrounded by a dozen charming maids

in pretty bathing costumes, made a very attractive sight. Miss Beckwith's tricks and fast swimming are worth journeying a long way to see."

August *Boston Globe, Boston Herald*: "It's dollars to doughnuts, they beat the world. This was the wager made by two members of the grand army of the Republic at the Aqueduct side in the Natatorium of the Grand Museum. The boys in blue were discussing the merits and her associates as professional swimmer. It is a fact that cannot be gainsaid that it would be impossible to drown this most fascinating water nymph, CLARA BECKWITH. New and novel features are being introduced daily. See the WATER KNIGHT'S TOURNAMENT, THE FUNNY DOUGNUT CHASE, THE SKIMMING PLATE, THE FOOTBALL MATCH. All accomplished by lovely ladies attired in sombre leotards in SALT WATER."

10 August *Boston Herald*: "Miss Clara Beckwith and her bath companions are billed for several novelties, foremost will be a grand tournament. Miss Beckwith will commander in chief and those who know her swimming powers will known how she will lead. The athlete, Miss Mary Duffin, will do the comic business and much fun can be expected in the 'doughnut chase', six lovely maidens all blindfolded, chasing around the doughnut, the successful one obtaining the gold medal."

16 August *New York Clipper*: "In the big tank at the Grand Museum Clara Beckwith and her bevy of female coadjutors cause unlimited fun by their feats and contests in the watery element and appear to be amphibious in their nature. Their "doughnut chase' in which six of the

girls compete blindfolded is brimful of comicality and causes roars of merriment.

24 August *Boston Herald*: "The aqueduct sensation of this coming week will be the appearance of Miss Clara Beckwith and Miss Mary Anderson in a series of life pictures representing the sports of Roman Gladiators."

23 September *Boston Globe*: "FAIR AQUATIC POLOISTS AT THE GRAND MUSEUM - Odd and Sensational performances offered for a Dime. Yale vs Harvards captained by Clara Beckwith, champion swimmer of the world proved most attractive at the 'Grand Museum'."

Boston Herald: "Water Polo, as exemplified at the Grand Museum, corner of Washington and Dover Streets, proved a decided novelty. The two teams, the Harvards and Yales, are captained by Miss Clara Beckwith and Katie Anderson and the bounding rubber ball was kept in constant motion until it was successfully hurled over the desired line of demarcation which constituted a desired goal. Both teams were dressed in appropriate costumes and the struggle of the diving and swimming maidens had the effect of exciting the large audience present up to a high state of enthusiasm."

24 September *New Haven Register*: "Lady Swimmers at the 'Grand Museum' have been playing polo in the water."

30 September *Boston Globe*: "In the natatorium Miss Clara Beckwith gave a wonderful exhibition of fancy swimming which attracted much attention."

1891 April *Boston Globe*, *Boston Evening Transcript*, *Boston Post* report that Clara Beckwith was performing at the Grand Museum in a continuous performance from 1 – 10:30 daily.

7 April *Boston Globe*: "Miss Clara Beckwith, queen of the Natatorium, (AT BOSTON GRAND MUSEUM) gave several exhibitions to the evident satisfaction of the visitors. Miss Beckwith's every movement is most graceful and she performs the most difficult athletic and aquatic feats with the greatest ease."

11 April *New York Clipper*: "Boston Grand Museum announces that Clara Beckwith, female swimmer and diver, is giving exhibitions in the great natatorium."

12 April *Boston Globe*: "In the big bath Miss Clara Beckwith holds full sway. Miss Beckwith has demonstrated her great ability in many exhibitions, and is willing to meet anyone who has an idea that they are her equal."

21 April *Boston Herald*: "In the natatorium, Miss Clara Beckwith, water witch, is still supreme as an attraction. The exhibition given by this lady has to be seen to be appreciated. Her feats under water are surprising."

July-August: Repeated notices in the *Lowell Courier* of Clara Beckwith offering daily exhibitions of her "various and extraordinary feats of fancy swimming" daily at 4:00pm at Lakeview.

August-November *New York Times* reports Clara Beckwith "disported herself in her swimming tank day and night" at 'Proctor's Theatre and Pleasure Palace.'"

1892 First national competitions for women swimming in Scotland.

Pursuing Clara

Printer's Ink volume 7, issue 24 discusses a Boston Alderman finding fault with a lithographed poster of Clara Beckwith in front of the 'Grand Museum'. "In the poster picture she wears dark tights and has her neck and arms bare. The Museum manager regards it as a work of art and will frame a copy and show it in his Museum."

November *Boston Globe*, *Boston Herald* report that Clara Beckwith, "Champion Lady Swimmer" is a regular attraction at Lothrup's Grand Museum.

8 November *Boston Herald*: "At the Grand Museum a special feature this week is the opening of the big natatorium which has been repaired and enlarged and will be devoted to aquatic sports and pastimes. This week, management introduce the charming water queen, Miss Clara Beckwith, who made so many friends at this house last season and the intricacy of her movements in the water are marvelous and a wonderment to all who witness her."

13 November *Boston Herald*: "CLARA BECKWITH - The most beautiful creature in the world. Graceful in form, pleasing in feature. Miss Beckwith is the result of one of nature's pleasing moods. Miss Beckwith, in her wonderful swimming feats the athlete equals the man of the world. She pleases the artist in form and grace. She makes ladies and children wonder how it is done. She accomplishes a 54 foot dive. She lives under water for three minutes; that is long enough to drown anybody. She waltzes, she does the sleeping beauty, the angel's prayer, the sacrifice and she eats her dinner and supper in the water. All this in the NATATORIUM OF THE GRAND MUSEUM."

27 November *Boston Herald*: "SPLASH, TERROR, DEATH - A splash means that daintily attired little affair will drop itself into the water. Terror means that the act will make you feel very uncomfortable. It is a human nature feeling. It comes over you because you think the poor creature is drowning. Death, well death means when you quit trouble. You will think that the gingerly trimmed little lady is drowned. You will think that her narrow little brain has gone to the bottom of the tar swabbed tank, or gone to her God, but it don't. She will blossom out as BECKWITH, the champion, the beautiful, the angelic at the Grand Museum."

December *Baltimore Sun*: "MISS BECKWITH IN THE SWIM - Commencing next Monday afternoon, Miss Clara Beckwith, champion lady natator of the world will give her phenomenal aquatic exhibition In the Monumental Theatre Annex Aquarium. This remarkable young lady performs the most astounding feats under the water."

1893 "IN THE SWIM – autobiography of MISS CLARA BECKWITH, World's Champion Lady Swimmer – The Theory and Practice of Swimming Explained and Illustrated by the MODERN MERMAID" printed by Wm U. Day in Baltimore, Maryland.

4 January *Baltimore Sun*: "Marvelous Aquatic feats by Clara Beckwith in the Annex."

15 January "Measurements of a Swimming Girl" first published in *Annals of Hygiene* (Volume 8) prepared and published by State Board of Health of Pennsylvania and republished in newspapers around the world, with the *Colorado Transcript* titling this "WHO MEASURED HER?"

18 January *Baltimore Sun*: Re-engagement announced of Miss Clara Beckwith giving swimming exhibitions in the Auditorium, at Kernan's Monumental Theatre.

20 February *Baltimore Sun*: Berselli's statue of Miss Clara Beckwith on exhibition in the foyer of the Howard Auditorium.

April *Baltimore Sun, New York Clipper, New York Dramatic Mirror* report Clara Beckwith giving daily aquatic exhibitions at upper wax hall of Howard Auditorium in Baltimore.

9 April *Baltimore Sunday Herald*: "A brilliant revival of Gilbert and Sullivan's popular opera 'H. M. S. Pinafore' will be this week's attraction at the Howard Auditorium commencing with the matinee tomorrow in conjunction with new and refined vaudeville features and the interesting and novel aquatic exhibitions of Miss Clara Beckwith, champion lady swimmer of the world. In the upper wax hall the aquatic exhibitions of Miss Clara Beckwith will be continued before and after the regular matinee and night performances. Admission to the swimming exhibition is only 10 cents, matinee daily."

20-24 May *Washington Bee, Kate Field's Washington* report Miss Clara Beckwith, champion lady swimmer of the world, as a special feature of 'Female Pedestrian Tournament' – 72 hours.

20 May *Washington Evening Star*: "Miss Clara Beckwith, Champion Lady Swimmer of the world will be a special card during the supplemental season, commencing June 5th with a female pedestrian tournament. Clara Beckwith been performing in Baltimore the previous six

months, eating, reading, and acting underwater, exhibitions at 3. 5, 9, 10 & 11, promising new and startling feats at every performance, farewell final performance on July 1st. Clara Beckwith gives exhibitions in a large tank in the theatre. A group of lights is places behind the tank so that every movement in the water may be seen by the audience....her imitation of how a person drowns is thrillingly interesting."

23 May *Washington Evening Star*: "Clara Beckwith the 'water queen' eats, reads and acts under water in full view of her audience at Kernan's theatre."

25/26 May *Washington Evening Star, New York Dramatic Mirror*: "Clara Beckwith, champion lady swimmer in the world will be introduced to the Washington amusement public at the Lyceum on June 5th."

30 May *Washington Evening Star*: "There is on exhibition at Kernan's Lyceum Theatre this week a plaster of paris model of Miss Clara Beckwith, the champion female swimmer of the world, whom M. De Berselli the wax worker at the Howard Auditorium, Baltimore, selected for his statue' The Diving Girl'. The model represents Miss Beckwith in typical bathing costume on the point of making a plunge. M. de Berselli does not claim originality for his work but was prompted to undertake the reproduction by the fact that Miss Beckwith afforded new opportunities to add grace and beauty to the subject. The Theatre will be open all week for the inspection of this work."

June *Washington Evening Star* and the *Washington Post*: "At the hours of 3, 5, 9, 10 and 11 Miss Clara Beckwith, champion lady swimmer gives exhibitions in a large tank in the theatre. A group of lights is placed behind the tank so that every movement in the water may be seen. The exhibition of Miss Beckwith is remarkable and her imitation of how a person drowns is thrillingly interesting."

Washington Post, New York Clipper, Washington Evening Star: Daily ads for female walking match at Kernans with Clara Beckwith.

10 June *Washington Evening Star*: "Miss Clara Beckwith's aquatic exhibitions will form the principal attraction at Kernan's Lyceum Theatre next week. The female pedestrians will rest from midnight tonight till Monday at 4:00 Monday afternoon when they will resume the 72 hours race which must be completed by12 pm on Saturday. Miss Beckwith appears at suitable intervals during the contest and as an indoor entertainment her performance serves to amuse patrons who have grown weary of the monotony of the track or to enliven the dull moments which are sure to occur in all walking matches. Miss Beckwith's feats under water are positively remarkable. She displays all the natatoroial facility of the fish combined with the grace and daring of the mermaid. Small as the aquarium is, she leaves no doubt of her high degree of skill. Ample evidence is given of this in her realistic imitation of a drowning woman."

22 June *Washington Post*, "It is with regret that Manager Kernan parts with Miss Clara Beckwith, champion lady swimmer of the world, after next week. She has proved a most entertaining feature in connection with

Ernest J. Dick

the walking match and will undoubtedly continue to be as popular and attractive entertaining in the fourth week of her engagement as she was in her first. The aquatic act has been watched with renewed interest week after week until it has been classed among the few acts now before the public that never lost its novelty."

24 June *Washington Evening Star*: "Miss Clara Beckwith will positively make her last appearance at Kernan's Lyceum Theatre in Washington next week. It is doubtful whether at any time in the history of this house a star has evoked more admiration than Miss Beckwith. Young, beautiful and graceful, with all the dexterity and daring of a fabulous mermaid she presents an act that possesses that novelty which never wears off. Her extended performance of four weeks is a new experience to the patrons though in Baltimore under James R., Kernan's management she appeared for over six months. Other engagements interfering, however Miss Beckwith cannot remain longer than next week. This should be born in mind as well as the hours of her appearance, 5, 9 & 10 pm."

July *New York Evening World, Chicago Daily Tribune, The World, New York Sun*: Daily notices of Clara Beckwith at Tony Pastor's.

1 July *Washington Evening Star*: "Close of Female Walking Match every day 4–6 and 8–12. Positively last appearance of Miss Clara Beckwith, champion Natataress of the World – The Slyph of the Sea at Kernan's."

5 July "Clara Beckwith the Star of 'Tony Pastor's' Program, the eight wonder of the world who can live, eat,

walk, play, waltz, read and act under water to appear at 'Tony Pastor's' next week."

8 July *The Evening World, New York Clipper*: "CLARA BECKWITH - the eighth wonder of the world who can live, eat, walk, play, waltz, read, and act under water" is performing at Tony Pastor's Theatre – New York. She will be seen in a glass tank 4 feet by 14 feet, 8 feet deep. Her appearance will be decidedly seasonable and her audience will probably be inclined to envy her luxury of a constant cold water bath."

New York Dramatic Mirror: "At the Lyceum Clara Beckwith has continued to be a drawing card in her remarkable aquatic performances. She is easily the most accomplished swimmer who ever appeared before Washington audiences. She opens at Tony Pastor's and is sure to be a popular attraction."

11 July *New York Herald*: "Tony Pastor introduced a seasonal novelty in Clara Beckwith, the expect lady swimmer whose exhibition was interesting and instructive. She gave exhibitions of eating and drinking under water and the struggles of a drowning person. The exhibition was given in a 10 by 5 foot tank and every movement was perceptible though the glass sides. At the end of the exhibition Miss Beckwith was presented with a basket of flowers."

15 July *Evening Star*: "Clara Beckwith, champion lady swimmer of the world performing at Kerman's Lyceum Theatre (Washington) in a tank 60 feet long erected in the summer garden, in place of the portable aquarium Miss Beckwith performed in earlier."

31 July *Lewiston Evening Journal*: "Clara Beckwith's feats in the water - Miss Clara Beckwith, who claims to be the champion lady swimmer of the world. She claims to have saved several people from drowning and to have swum 74 ½ miles in six days. She also declares that she can remain under water for over 2 ½ minutes, which is certainly a very remarkable performance."

August *Washington Evening Star, Washington Post*: Daily ads for Clara Beckwith, Slyph of the Sea, Zephyr of the Sea, appearing at Kernan's.

5 August *Washington Evening Star, Topeka Daily Capital*: Special feature in the garden section on Miss Clara Beckwith, Sylph of the Sea.

6 August *Chicago Daily Tribune*: *Clara Beckwith*, Champion lady swimmer, reported to enter some of the races at the Mattison.

12 August *New York Dramatic Mirror*: "Clara Beckwith the shapely and accomplished lady swimmer as a side attraction. A new tank 60 feet long has been especially erected for her in the summer garden accompanying the Lyceum where she will perform her incomparable feats."

16 August *Waterloo Daily Courier* runs "Clara Beckwith's Feats in Water", an abbreviation of part of *In the Swim*. It concludes: "The one thing Miss Beckwith cannot admire in the American girl is the fact that she very rarely learns to swim. In England, according to Miss Beckwith, three-fourths of the women can swim."

26 August *New York Dramatic Mirror*: "After the regular performance in the theatre, Clara Beckwith will give

her remarkable swimming exhibitions in the large tank in the summer garden adjoining the theatre."

31 August *Washington Evening Star*: "Positively the last week of Miss Clara Beckwith in her natatorial diversions".

1 September Wilbert W. Clarke marries Harriet L. Hardwicke in Annapolis Royal.

9 September *San Francisco Chronicle*: *Clara Beckwith* expected to visit the Crystal Baths.

16 September *New York Clipper*: *Clara Beckwith* at Sommer Park in Montreal.

25 September *Montreal Daily Witness*: "*Clara Beckwith* made her last appearance at the Laurentian Bath on Saturday last. The attendance was the largest of the week. The competitors in Mr. Saikeld's programme exceeded that of any previous entertainments."

October-November *New York Times, The Evening World, New York Tribune, New York Herald, New York Sun*: "Clara Beckwith, the Water Queen" at Tony Pastor's Theatre, lives, eats, waltzes, plays, reads, acts, underwater, eight wonder of the world."

12 November *Boston Post*: "A Mermaid's Hint to Beginners" includes image of Clara Beckwith doing a handstand from *In the Swim*, and repeats instructions on how to learn to swim and how to stand on your hands in water.

November-December *Kalamazoo Gazette, Evansville Courier and Press, Buffalo Evening News*: "Swimming is Good" is a reprint of "A Mermaid's Hint to Beginners" from *In the Swim*.

Ernest J. Dick

1894 23 January *Bismark Daily Tribune*, reprinting from the *Boston Post*: "How to Swim: There is no difficulty in learning how to swim, says Clara Beckwith. Amongst the greatest benefits I have derived from swimming is the remarkable preservation of my health in all seasons and under all conditions of changing climate, diet and surroundings."

24 June *Washington Post*: Theatrical chat column discusses "Living Pictures" discussing whether these were real of faked "Another man declared that the living picture of the diver was nothing more or less than the plaster cast of Clara Beckwith, the swimmer who was at Kernan's last summer."

August *Washington Times, Evening Star*: Clara Beckwith, said to be the "bewitching, captivating water nymph" performing at Kernan's Lyceum Theatre.

Washington Evening Star, New York Clipper: "Kernan's Lyceum Theatre, home of vaudeville, commences the season with Frank M. Mills Vaudeville Co and living pictures...The unique attraction that drew an immense throng to River View Sunday comprised George Whistler's clever nautical exhibitions, a grand nautical battle on the water, complete destruction of vessels by torpedoes, throwing a mass of water hundreds of feet in the air, walking on water, riding a bicycle on water, exhibition of a shipwreck at sea; and cooking his meals and eating with Captain Webb's performing seals, prairie dog village and educated alligators. Clara Beckwith, the swimmer, commences a three-week engagement at Kernam's Lyceum to giving exhibitions in the big swimming pool especially erected in the summer garden attached."

New York Evening Star, New York Dramatic Mirror, Washington Post: "Miss Clara Beckwith, charming water nymph, continues her exhibitions in the summer garden."

September *New York Clipper*: Clara Beckwith continuing her performances at Kernan's.

1895 22 May *New York Herald*: Clara Beckwith to swim on behalf of pension fund of Pilots Benevolent Association at 5th Ave Theatre with her tank and all of her apparatus.

June *New York Herald*: Clara Beckwith, champion lady swimmer will give her interesting aquatic demonstrations for Pilots Benevolent Association.

2 June *New York Herald*: Summary of Clara's career clearly taken from her 'Autobiography', particularly the three life-saving stories, and explains how she will demonstrate saving people from drowning. "This exhibition will be given in a huge glass tank, containing many hundreds of gallons of water that has been shipped from Boston and will be placed on stage of the Fifth Ave Theatre the evening before the performance. Miss Beckwith was among the first to offer the pilots her services and will travel a long distance to be present and offer her share of the entertainment."

14 June *Trenton Times*: Clara Beckwith telling people how to learn to swim.

15 June *New York Clipper*: "Clara Beckwith performed interesting feats underwater to conclude the acts at the 'Fifth Avenue Theatre' for the Sandy Hook Pilots' Benevolent Association."

Ernest J. Dick

August 1895 *New York Times*, *New York Post*: Clara Beckwith, famous sensational swimmer, performing in Proctor's continuous show.

18 August *New York Times*: Ad for Clara Beckwith at Proctors.

20 August *New York Herald*: "Miss Clara Beckwith, the swimmer, was ill and her appearance was postponed."

25 August Clara Beckwith, charming water nymph, continues exhibitions at summer garden of Kernan's Lyceum Theatre.

31 August *New York Dramatic Mirror*: "Frank Hall's Casino in Chicago has closed a contract with *Cora Beckwith* to float in a mammoth tank of water for 40 days for a purse of $1500."

New York Clipper: *Clara Beckwith* listed as appearing at Toronto Industrial Fair and Montreal Sommer Park.

7 September 1895 *New York Dramatic Mirror*: *Clara Beckwith*, the English mermaid retained for third week at Sommer Park in Montreal.

12 September Toronto *Daily Mail and Empire*: "*Miss Clara Beckwith*, the fancy swimmer whose wonderful tank performance has so much enhanced the water fête, will go to Baltimore at the close of the Fair. She has secured a 16 weeks engagement in that city."

24 October *New York Times, New York Dramatic Mirror*: Clara Beckwith performing at Proctor's Pleasure Palace in tank.

November *Good Health Magazine*, published by Kellogg in Battle Creek, Michigan includes short article by Clara Beckwith entitled 'Learning to Swim'.

Pursuing Clara

New York Dramatic Mirror: "Clara Beckwith, Champion swimmer, at Proctor's performing wonderful feats under water".

10 November *New York Herald*: "Standing room only, and not much of that, at Proctor's for continuous show including Clara Beckwith showing how much she was at home in the water."

16 November New York Dramatic Mirror: "*Clara Beckwith*, Champion Lady Swimmer who recently accomplished the feat of floating for 40 days in a tank at the Casino, Chicago, has an engagement to appear at the Atlantic Exposition."

"Clara Beckwith, expert swimmer, was expecting to begin her performance at Proctor's Pleasure Palace three weeks ago but is being compelled to rest because her tank was lost by the railway company and has been found at some out of the way place. She will be suing the railway company for her enforced idleness."

17 November *The Sun*: Clara Beckwith swimming in a glass tank at Proctor's.

19 November *New York Times*, *New York Tribune*: "New entertainers, including Clara Beckwith and her 'tank exploits' at Proctor's Pleasure Palace, ate, drank, sewed and disported herself, between George Lochart's elephants and a burlesque bullfight."

New York Times, New York Herald: Clara Beckwith, in her swimming tank appearing day and night at Proctor's Pleasure Palace.

25 November 16-page program for Proctor's Pleasure Palace (full-colour front and rear) with Clara Beckwith and her 'tank exploits' listed.

December *New York Herald, New York Dramatic Mirror*: Clara Beckwith reported swimming at Proctor's Pleasure Palace.

1896 February New York Herald, New York Tribune, New York Dramatic Mirror: Clara Beckwith in her daring aquatic sports at Proctor's.

22 February *New York Dramatic Mirror*: "Clara Beckwith offered swimming exhibitions at the New Manhattan Athletic Club on the occasion of the 28th anniversary of the formation of Benevolent and Protective Order of Elks (entertainments beginning at noon and lasting until midnight) with 8,000 members and visitors present and including sword contests, juggling, feats of strength, boxing, gymnastics and music"

14 March *New York Dramatic Mirror*: Jake Rosenthal of Chicago reported as organizing good time for *Clara Beckwith*, the swimmer.

3 July *Daily Nor'Wester* and *Winnipeg Free Press*: "The platform attractions of the Manitoba Industrial Exhibition this year are better arranged than ever. The Skatorial Trio will give their grotesque elephant act; Messrs Rice and Elmer will appear in their comedy triple entertainment; dancing of the most fancy and novel character will be done by the Coulson sisters: Clara Beckwith, the renowned aquatorial artist, will give astonishing feats in water."

3 August 1896 *The Press*: *Clara Beckwith*, champion swimmer, is said to be giving exhibitions daily at Old Point Comfort.

1897 23 July Theodore C. Tebbetts married to Helen V. Curtis in Detroit, Michigan.

6 August *Daily Nor'Wester*: "There were on the train from Brandon this morning the Nelson Sisters, Porter Bros, Miss Clara Beckwith, Prof Blink and his performing dogs all of whom were on the programme of attractions at the Industrial exhibition here and afterwards went to Brandon to entertain there during fair week."

8 November *Daily Nor'Wester*: Clara M. Beckwith of Baltimore reported as staying at the Manitoba Hotel.

1898 7 February *Baltimore Sun*: The engagement is announced of Miss Clara Beckwith of 926 North Fulton Ave., Baltimore to Dr. S. W. McInnis of Brandon, Manitoba.

23 February *Cincinnati Post*: Marriage license issued to Clara M. Beckwith and Stanley W. McInnis of the Grand Hotel.

Clara May Beckwith marries Stanley Wm McInnis in Hamilton County, Ohio.

15 October Carrie Hardwicke arrives in Boston aboard 'SS Prince Edward'.

1899 3 March Joshua M Sabean (Clara's father) dies in Boston, listed as labourer.

28 March *New York Tribune*: *Clara Beckwith* appeared as dancer at Pleasure Palace.

2 April *New York Herald*: *Clara Beckwith* at Proctor's.

1900 1 April *Denver Post*: Tilie Ashford, born in Norway, and eventually becoming competitive swimmer, said to be taking lessons from *Clara Beckwith*.

14 June Clement Miller, musician, age 33, living at home with parents as musician at 50 Temple St., Boston. (US census).

1901 Clara M McInnis (said to be born in 1873 and immigrating from Britain in 1887) living with Stanley McInnis, 2 domestics and 7-year old son William Stuckey in Brandon (Canadian Census).

1904 23 January *Brandon Daily Sun*: "Mrs. McInnis poured tea and coffee from 4 – 5 at the social event of the season saying good-by to Mrs. J. C Nichol leaving Brandon for New York".

12 April *Brandon Daily Sun*: Mrs. S. W. McInnis included as a patroness of a bachelors' 'at home'.

1905 Annette Kellerman enters an annual swimming race in Paris, said to be the first women to enter a race against men and half a million people line the banks of the river to witness the race. Later that summer Annette Kellerman becomes the first woman to attempt to swim the English Channel. She develops a swimming and diving act which she performs in a glass tank on stage at the London Hippodrome and draws large crowds.

1907 Annette Kellerman doing synchronized swimming at New York Hippodrome, arrested for indecency.

5 November *Manitoba Free Press*: "Foremost Citizen of Brandon Passed Away After Brief Illness - He was conscious up to the last and passed away as he had lain all day, without suffering any pain. His wife was at his bedside constantly, throughout the day, most of which was spent in conversation between the two as if nothing was happening, but it has been since declared that he was advising Mrs. McInnis what to do after he passed away."

Photograph of Mrs. Stanley McInnis in *Brandon Daily Sun* (see p.64) together with proclamation of mayor proclaiming November 7th as public holiday so that all citizens can attend the funeral of Stanley McInnis.

18 November Clara McInnis disbursed $300 from McInnis Estate.

29 November Clara McInnis disbursed $100 from McInnis Estate.

1908 25 January Clara McInnis disbursed $100 from McInnis Estate.

20 February Clara McInnis disbursed $12 for travel expenses from McInnis Estate.

2 March Clara McInnis disbursed $100 from McInnis Estate

2 June Clara's sister, Annie Sabine, dies in Boston, birthplace given as Bridgeton, Maine, with father Mannings Sabine and mother Jane Wade, both born in Bridgeton, Maine (buried at Mt Hope Cemetery Section F – grave 2214).

10 June Clara McInnis disbursed $100 from McInnis Estate

25 November Clara M. McInnis, age 36, maiden name Clara Beckwith (born in England), daughter of Manning Beckwith and Abbie J. Wade, married to Clement G. Miller, musician, age 41 at People Temple Methodist Church in Suffolk, Boston.

18 December Clara McInnis disbursed $100 from McInnis Estate.

1909 13 January *Annapolis Spectator*: "Mrs. C.M. McInnis travels to Montreal, leaving orders to have the Ritchie

Ernest J. Dick

mansion in Annapolis Royal fitted up for her occupancy. It is generally understood that she has purchased the property."

8 February Clara McInnis purchases St. Andrews School property (described as 494 St. George Street) in Annapolis Royal from Joseph F. Foster Estate for $3,000 (deed book # 142, p 56).

11 February Clara McInnis transfers 494 St. George Street to Caroline A. Hardwick, spinster from Boston, Mass for $2,000.

17 February *Annapolis Spectator*: Mrs. McInnis travels to Brandon, Manitoba.

26 February Clara McInnis disbursed $100 from Mcinnis Estate.

16 June *Annapolis Spectator*: Mrs. McInnis returns from trip to Boston; and Mrs. S. W. McInnis will receive from 8 to 10 on Friday evening next, June 18.

June-July *Annapolis Spectator*: Ads for 'Old Orchard House' "offering beautiful grounds, airy rooms, modern equipment, fishing, boating, bathing, tennis and good service" from C. M. McInnis.

September Mrs. Stanley W. McInnis, described as being of Scotch origin, born in Annapolis Royal, arriving at St. Alban's, Vermont from Yarmouth, Nova Scotia, birth date given as 1872 (Church of Jesus Christ of Latter-day Saints web-site "United States Border Crossings from Canada").

13 September Clara McInnis sells 494 St. George Street to Josephine Mills of Annapolis Royal for $1500, subject to a $2,000 mortgage.

Pursuing Clara

2 November Annapolis Royal Town Council minutes record town policeman, Conlin, being asked why he has not arrested Mrs McInnis..

1910 24 April US Census has Clara (McInnis/Beckwith) Miller (said to be born in 1874 in England and immigrating in 1890), most recently from Brandon, Manitoba, living with Clement G Miller, musician, at 228 Huntington Ave. in the country of Suffolk, (father Manning Beckwith and mother Abbie J. Wade).

1911 25 June Clara McInnis disbursed $1000 from McInnis estate.

1912 25 October Clara McInnis disbursed $50 from McInnis Estate.

29 October Clara McInnis disbursed $25 from McInnis Estate.

1 November Clara McInnis disbursed $2210 from McInnis Estate.

1913 14 June Clara McInnis disbursed $648 from McInnis Estate.

2 August *Ogden Standard*: Article on women swimmers suggests that *Clara Beckwith* swimming 20 miles in six hours on the Thames in 1878 is the longest swim on record.

23 November Clara McInnis disbursed $102.50 from McInnis Estate.

1914 9 January McInnis disbursed $180 from McInnis Estate.

29 January Clara McInnis disbursed $304.50 from McInnis Estate.

19 March Clara McInnis Miller disbursed from McInnis Estate.

16 November Clara McInnis Miller disbursed $1000 from McInnis Estate.

1915 *Boston City Directory*: Clement Miller living at 115 Norway as musician.

16 November Clara Miller of Boston acknowledged as beneficiary of McInnis Estate.

18 November $997.15 bank draft purchased from McInnis Estate in favour of Mrs Clara Miller and F. Forbush.

6 December John E Regan served Clara Miller before notary public in Massachusetts.

1916 Clement G. Miller enlists as private with 17th infantry.

23 October Clara's mother, Jane Sabean, dies at 70 Palmer St in Boston, buried in Mt. Hope Cemetery.

1917 18 February Clara McInnis Miller paid annuity of $1005.41 from Stanley W. McInnis Estate for 1916.

4 August *Clara Beckwith*'s balloon ascension, double somersaults in the air, and parachute leaps were last weeks' special attraction at Broad Ripple Park in Indianapolis

October *Clara Beckwith* offering balloon ascensions, with triple parachute drops by lady aeronaut, now giving 643 South Fair Street, Indianapolis as her address.

1918 Annette Kellerman publishes *How to Swim.*

10 April Clara McInnis Miller disbursed $1000 from McInnis Estate.

19 December Clara McInnis Miller disbursed $1000 from McInnis Estate.

1919 5 March Caroline Hardwicke, born 1876 in Annapolis, dies in Suffolk, Massachusetts of tuberculosis, age 43, working as teacher, buried in Annapolis Royal.
28 November 1919 Clara McInnis Miller disbursed $1000 from McInnis Estate.
1920 January Clara Miller is 37, widowed, born in Maryland, with parents from England, can read and write, and is living with the Tebbetts family as a servant at 37 Baltimore Street, Lynn, Massachusetts, according to the US census.

Clement G. Miller is renting and living at 111 Norway Street, divorced, working as musician, in precinct 8, Suffolk County, Boston according to the US census.

26 July Theodore Charles Tebbetts, born 1871 (wife – Virginia Curtis), living at 37 Baltimore St., Lynn, Mass, dies and is buried in Pine Grove Cemetery, Lynn, Massacussetts.

27 July *Boston Herald*: "Lynn Man ends life by Bullet"

10 November Clara McInnis Miller disbursed $1000 McInnis Estate.
1921 18 November Clara McInnis Miller disbursed $1000 from McInnis Estate.
1922 3 August George Lothrup dies.

1 November Clara McInnis Miller disbursed $1000 from McInnis Estate.
1923 9 July *Ogden Standard-Examiner, Lincoln Star*: Announcement of Clara Miller, sales women for oil syndicate of Los Angeles, receiving a bequest of $250,000 from estate of Tebbetts.

9 July *Lewiston Daily Sun*: "Doubt, reported gift of one quarter million - Mrs. Helen Tebbetts, widow of Theodore Tebbetts said that she knew of no such person as Mrs.

Miller. The estate to be divided between members of the surviving family and a number of private bequests ....Mrs. Clara Miller, saleswomen for an oil syndicate, has announced receipt of a letter from a Boston law firm telling her that she has been left $250,000 in the will of Theodore Tebetts."

10 July *New York Times*: "Tells of $250 Legacy" New York Times letter from Boston legal firm re Clara May Miller being left $250,000 - to go to Boston where will is being probated.... Young Tebbetts father gave her $1,000 to buy clothes to replaces those ruined in saving his son, she said, and the Canadian authorities gave her a medal for heroism."

10 July *New Castle News*: "Tells of $250,000 Legacy" Mrs. Miller, then Clara Beckwith, rescues lad in Bay of Fundy 35 years earlier.

11 July *Boston Herald*: "Denys Tebbetts Left Women $250,000 – Helen Tebbetts explaining that Clara Miller was a good cook but had to discharge her for other reasons. 'I don't think she ever saw Mr Tebbetts in her life. At the time she claims to have saved his life when he fell off a boat in the Bay of Fundy, we were married and travelling in England."

13 November Clara McInnis Miller disbursed $993.98 from McInnis Estate.

1924 Historical Association of Annapolis Royal publishes *The Romance of Old Annapolis Royal* by Charlotte Perkins.

16 February *New York Clipper*: Cora Beckwith dies as Mrs. Jake Rosenthal at the age 48, owning several acts

that perform with her. She is said to be of the Beckwiths of Lambeth and beginning her career at age of 9.

1925 19 December $200 wired to Clara Miller in Santa Monica, California from McInnis Estate.

23 December 1925 $100 wired to Clara Miller in Santa Monica, California from McInnis Estate.

23 December $269.64 paid to Munson, All & co re judgment re Clara Miller from McInnis Estate.

1926 2 January $150 wired to Clara Miller in Santa Monica, California from McInnis Estate.

15 January $46.05 payment to County Court re judgment of Clara Miller at Empire Hotel from McInnis Estate.

$1000 claim against Clara Miller paid to Mrs. L. Merriam from McInnis Estate, followed by many other claims from various sources.

11 November $148 disbursed to Clara Miller from McInnis Estate.

12 November $152.75 paid in claim against Clara Miller from McInnis Estate.

1927 11 November $148 disbursed to Clara Miller from McInnis Estate.

1928 23 June $353.56 paid to N Tripp & Co, California due Clara Miller from McInnis Estate.

22 November $1000 disbursed to Clara Miller from McInnis estate.

1929 14 November $1000 disbursed to Clara Miller from McInnis Estate.

1930 7 April Clement G. Miller, divorced and living and renting at 99 Norway, Street, Boston, Suffolk County, according to US Census.

25 November $998.70 disbursed to Clara Miller from McInnis Estate.

Ernest J. Dick

1931 26 February Clara M Miller swears legal affidavit in Boston legal office of Norman Trippe – Forbush and Trippe at 53 State Street in Boston.
1932 4 November $1,000 due C Miller from McInnis Estate paid to C. M Miller and Siloon Merriam.
1933 17 November $1,000 due C Miller from McInnis Estate paid to C. M Miller and Siloon Merriam.
1934 12 November $1,000 due C Miller from McInnis Estate paid to C. M Miller and Siloon Merriam.
1935 12 November $1,000 due C Miller from McInnis Estate paid to C. M Miller and Siloon Merriam - $900 paid less $100 tax.
1936 9 November $1,000 due C Miller from McInnis Estate paid to Myron P. Lewis - $950 paid less $50 tax
1937 5 March *Cleveland Plain Dealer*: Clement Miller students took part in recital as part of alumnae recital.

9 November $1,000 due C Miller from McInnis Estate and paid to Myron P. Lewis - $950 paid less $50 tax.
1938 4 November $1,000 due C Miller from McInnis Estate and paid to Myron P. Lewis - $950 paid less $50 tax.
1939 7 November $1,000 due C Miller from McInnis Estate paid to E Larsen - $950 paid less $50 tax.
1940 13 March $399 disbursed to Clara Miller from McInnis Estate.

3 April Clara M Miller, widowed and head of household renting at 79 Warren, Boston, living with Bertha Burgess (nurse) and lodger Eliza Morse, according to US census. Clara is also said to be working 84 hours a week as a nurse, 52 weeks of the year, in the census report.

16 April US Census has a Clara M Miller living as a patient in the Boston State Hospital.

6 November $1,000 due C Miller from McInnis Estate paid to E. Larsen - $950 paid less $50 tax.

Pursuing Clara

1941 5 February $140 disbursed to Clara Miller from McInnis Estate.

12 December $420 disbursed to Clara Miller from McInnis Estate.

1942 16 January $490 disbursed to Clara Miller from McInnis Estate.

9 November $1,000 due C Miller from McInnis Estate and paid to E. Larsen, $850 paid less $150 non-resident tax.

15 December $435.00 disbursed to Clara Miller from McInnis Estate.

1943 31 May Clara McInnis dies, according to Stanley McInnis probate records and confirmed by death certificate, while living at 79 Warren with next of kin listed as Boston Public Welfare.

23 November Letter from Boston legal firm confirming Clara McInnis Miller died leaving no will, assets or relatives.

8 December Balance of $230 of disbursed from McInnis Estate paid to E. Larsen.

1948 25 January Clement G. Miller, musician, dies while living in the Tetland Masonic Lodge (where he was initiated in 1894), maybe buried at Pine Grove Cemetery, Gilmonton Ironworks, New Hampshire.

'Easy Pieces # 5, an Old Court Dance', 1 minute 30 seconds for piano, score by J. Fisher, dedicated to Clement Miller.

Ernest J. Dick

About the author

Ern Dick is an archivist, oral historian, lecturer, and student of the sound and moving image of Atlantic Canada—and now is becoming an historical detective. He was originally from a fruit and vegetable farm in south-western Ontario, worked for the Public Archives of Canada and as Corporate Archivist of the Canadian Broadcasting Corporation in Ottawa, and has been living in Granville Ferry, Nova Scotia for the past 25 years.

Figure 17: Ern Dick at the CBC

Ern has worked with museums, broadcasting, heritage societies large and small, friends and neighbours to animate the past—always following the stories the past has to tell.

Notes

Ernest J. Dick

1. Jim How and Charlotte Perkins in conversation: https://tinyurl.com/y5asg3zw.
2. *Annapolis Spectator*, 25 April, 1935.
3. David Day and Margaret Roberts, *Swimming Communities in Victorian England*. London: Palgrave Press, 2019,
4. Catharine Esther Beecher, *Physiology and Calisthenics for Schools and Families*. New York: Harper & Brothers, 1856.
5. *Boston Globe*, 3 February, 1889.
6. *Boston Globe*, 4 July, 1889.
7. *Ibid.*
8. *Boston Herald*, 21 July, 1889.
9. *Boston Herald*, 19 July, 1889.
10. *Boston Herald*, 28 July, 1889.
11. *Printer's Ink*, volume 7, issue 24, 1892.
12. *Boston Herald*, 17 August, 1889,
13. *Boston Globe*, 25 September, 1889.
14. *Boston Daily Advertiser*, 27 May, 1890.
15. *Boston Globe*, 23 September, 1890.
16. *Boston Herald*, 27 November, 1892.
17. *Washington Post*, 24 June, 1894.
18. *Washington Evening Star*, 6 June, 1893.
19. *Washington Evening Star*, 24 June, 1893.
20. *The Evening World*, 8 July, 1893.
21. *New York Dramatic Mirror*, 16 November, 1895.
22. *Manitoba Free Press*, 7 November 1907.
23. Ian Lawrence, *Historic Annapolis Royal: Images of our Past*, Halifax: Nimbus, 2002.
24. *Boston Herald*, 1 July, 1920.
25. *Boston Herald*, 11 July, 1923.
26. Bird, *These are the Maritimes*.
27. *Weekly Journal or British Gazetteer*, October 5, 1728; November 23, 1728; *Daily Post*, June 6, 1732; Census 1871 RG101487: 2; Dahn Shaulis, 'Pedestriennes: Newsworthy but Controversial Women in Sporting Entertainment, *Journal of Sport History*, 26, no.1 (1999): 31-35; Kathleen E. McCrone, 'Class, Gender, and English Women's Sport, c. 1890-1914', *Journal of Sport History*, 18, no. 1 (1991): 166.
28. Robert Watson, 'Comparative Generations', in *Swimmers and Swimming or, The Swimmers Album*, Charles Newman (London, Henry Kemshead, 1899), 22; British Library *Evan* 645. *Canterbury Theatre of Varieties*, October 14, 1889; *Era*,

January 5, 1889, 25; 23 August 23, 1890, 22; April 21, 1894, 26; *Penny Illustrated*, March 5 1887, 151; *Bell's Life in London and Sporting Chronicle*, September 29, 1883, 11; June 23, 1885, 4.

29 *Manchester Times*, September 21, 1900, 8; *Daily News*, December 20, 1889, 3; *Licensed Victuallers' Mirror*, April 15, 1890, 174; Census Returns. Easton 1881 (337/61/1818), 1891 (141/84/67), 1901 (1253/76/40), 1911.

30 *Era*, June 14, 1884, 5; *Penny Illustrated*, May 27, 1876, 10; July 19, 1884, 2, 6; *Fun*, August 6, 1884, 57; Agnes Alice Beckwith, GRO (1861/birth/September/Lambeth/1d/319) born 14 August.

31 Pierre Bourdieu, *Practical Reason: On the Theory of Action* (Cambridge: Polity Press, 1998); C. Wright Mills, *The Sociological Imagination* (Harmondsworth: Penguin, 1970), 12; E. P. Thompson, *The Making of the English Working Class* (New York: Random House, 1963).

32 *Manchester Guardian*, September 2, 1875, 8; *Freeman's Journal and Daily Commercial Advertiser*, September 3, 1875, 2; *New York Times*, September 18, 1875, 12; *North Otago Times*, November 25 1875, 5; *Grey River Argus*, November 9, 1875, 2.

33 *Newcastle Courant*, May 5, 1876, 5; *Daily News*, July 6 1876, 3; *New York Times*, July 18 1876, 8 citing the *London Echo*, July 6, 1876; *Otago Witness*, September 9, 1876, 17; September 30, 1876, 5.

34 *Penny Illustrated*, July 27, 1878, 14; *Bell's Life*, August 10, 1878, 12.

35 *Bells Life*, May 8, 1880, 8; May 15, 1880, 12; *Reynolds's Newspaper*, May 9, 1880, 8-9; *Inter Ocean*, May 29, 1880; *Evening Post*, July 12, 1880, 2; British Library. Evan. 2756 London Westminster Royal Aquarium 1880 Poster.

36 *Bell's Life*, June 26, 1880, 8-9; July 3, 1880, 8; *Lloyd's Weekly Newspaper*, June 27, 1880, 5; July 4, 1880, 1; *Bristol Mercury and Daily Post*, July 3, 1880, 6.

37 *The Times*, August 26, 1879, 9; *Penny Illustrated*, August 30, 1879, 10; *Graphic*, August 30, 1879, 211; *Northern Echo*, August 20, 1894, 3; *Bell's Life*, September 27, 1879, 5.

38 *Era*, January 26, 1868, 16; March 29, 1868, 11; *Liverpool Mercury*, February 15, 1868, 6; *Penny Illustrated*, June 19, 1869), 391; *Bell's Life*, September 21, 1870, 4; July 22, 1871, 9; *Era*, February 4, 1872, 10; August 18, 1872, 5.

39 *Baily's Monthly Magazine of Sports and Pastimes*, April 1884, XLII(290): 183; *Swimming Notes*, May 3, 1884, 8; *Bell's Life*, August 17, 1872, 6; September 26, 1874, 8; November 14,

1874, 8; *Era*, August 18, 1872, 5; May 4 1873, 7; May 18, 1873, 3; June 1, 1873, 3; August 10, 1873, 3; August 17, 1873, 3; November 9, 1873, 3.

40 Agnes Alice Beckwith GRO (1882/marriage/March/Lambeth/1d/520). Census Returns 1891 (394/27/12), 1901 (383/89/3).

41 *Penny Illustrated*, May 5, 1883, 279; August 18, 1883, 10; *Reynolds's Newspaper*, May 13, 1883, 8; *New York Times*, June 5, 1883, 2; *Macon Weekly Telegraph,* September 30 1883, 6; *New York Clipper*, June 16, 1883), 208; *Bell's Life*, May 6, 1882, 6; *Liverpool Mercury*, February 8, 1887, 5; *Era*, March 5, 1887, 16; *New York Clipper*, April 23, 1887, 94; *Lancaster Daily Intelligencer*, April 2, 1887, 4.

42 *Era*, January 1, 1898, 22; January 29, 1898, 20, 22; January 21, 1899, 20; *Lloyd's Weekly Newspaper*, December 24, 1899, 13.

43 *Daily Mirror*, August 8, 1904, 2; August 10, 1904, 2; August 22, 1904, 2; September 21, 1904, 10; September 23, 1904, 10; *Bath Chronicle and Weekly Gazette*, December 31, 1908, 3; *Manchester Guardian*, June 20, 1910, 1; June 23, 1910, 1; June 24, 1910, 1; June 25, 1910, 1; June 27, 1910, 1; June 28, 1910, 1; Census 1911

44 GRO (1916/marriage/July/Exeter/5b/174); GRO (1941/death/October/Surrey/2a/443); Principal Probate Registry of England and Wales, Llandudno, March 1942; Manifest List for Union Castle Line, The Carnarvon Castle departing Southampton 31 August 1948; Nazareth House Records.

45 *Bell's Life*, May 4, 1886, 1; May 25, 1886, 1; *Era*, June 15, 1889, 15; June 7, 1890; August 29, 1891, 15; September 5, 1891, 8; *Northern Echo*, August 12, 1890, 4; *Licensed Victuallers' Mirror*, October 13, 1891, 490; *Horse and Hound, A Journal of Sport and Agriculture*, September 23, 1893, 593.

46 *Era*, June 23, 1888, 15; May 25, 1889, 20; August 10, 1889, 7; September 12, 1896, 21; September 19, 1896, 19; September 26, 1896, 20; October 3, 1896, 22; October 24, 1896, 31; November 7, 1896, 28; November 14, 1896, 23; December 5, 1896, 31, 32; January 23, 1897, 22, 29; February 6, 1897, 16; February 13, 1897, 15, 19; September 11, 1897, 15; November 27, 1897, 14, 30; December 11, 1897, 26; December 25, 1897, 21; January 8, 1898, 9; February 5, 1898, 29; February 12, 1898, 19; February 19, 1898, 24; February 26, 1898, 19, 20; April 2, 1898, 34; May 21, 1898, 26.

47 Manifest List for S.S. Umbria arriving in New York July 1904; *Morning Telegraph*, September 30, 1904, 6; *Daily Mirror*, March 1, 1905, 6; *Nottingham Evening Post*, March 4, 1905, 6.

48 *Era*, June 10, 1899, 19. GRO Agnes Harriett Beckwith (1884/birth/December/Lambeth/1d/367). Census 1891 (393/58/37). GRO (1884/marriage/June/Chelsea/1a/579) Charles Beckwith, 23, teacher of swimming, Emily Beckwith, 24, Agnes Beckwith, 6, Charles Beckwith, 4.

49 Newman, *Swimmers or Swimming or, The Swimmers Album*; GRO (1877/marriage/December/Lambeth/1d/688); Census 1891 (391/132/7) 281 Kennington Road, Lambeth, William H. Beckwith, 33, professional swimmer, Emma Beckwith Wife, 33, Frederick E. Beckwith Son, 4; *Era*, July 30, 1892; August 6, 1892, 22. Emma, Willie and son Frederick appeared together at Scarborough alongside Olivette Flower.

50 *Era*, October 5, 1895, 12; October 19, 1895, 7; February 1, 1896, 16; February 29, 1896, 8; March 7, 1896, 21; May 9, 1896, 23; October 10, 1896, 22; January 23, 1897, 29; May 8, 1897, 20; February 27, 1897, 23; May 25, 1889, 20; July 4, 1891, 16; September 26, 1896, 21.

51 *Boston Herald*, November 6, 1888, 3/8; *Star*, March 6, 1889, 3.

52 The Library and Archives Canada. 1871 Census, Clarence, Annapolis, Nova Scotia; Roll, C-10543; Page#6; Family No, 21; 1881 Census, New Caledonia, Annapolis, Nova Scotia; Roll, C-13172; Page#6; Family No, 27.

53 Charlotte Isabella Perkins, *The Romance of Old Annapolis Royal, Nova Scotia*, 1934, revised 1952.

54 *New York Clipper*, August 10, 1888-1890, 355; *Poughkeepsie Daily Eagle*, September 26, 1889, 2; *New York Times*, September 28, 1889.

55 *New York Clipper*, August 9, 1890, 342; *Boston Daily Globe*, September 23, 1890, 2; *Lowell Daily Courier*, June 30, 1891; July 8, 1891; July 16, 1891; August 10, 1891.

56 *Washington Bee*, May 20, 1893; *The Sun*, July 17, 1893, 8; October 29, 1893, 3; *Evening Telegram*, July 18, 1893, 4; *New York Times*, October 29, 1893; *New York Daily Tribune*, October 29, 1893, 22; *Washington Times*, August 14, 1894, 3.

57 *New York Times*, August 18, 1895, 11; October 24, 1895, 13; November 3, 1895; November 24, 1895, 12; *Era*, August 24, 1895; October 26, 1895; November 9, 1895; *New York Daily Tribune*, November 19, 1895, 5; *New York Times*, November 19, 1895, 5; *The Sun*, November 24, 1895, 3; *Spirit of the Times*, December 21, 1895, 752; *New York Dramatic Mirror*, December 21, 1895, 19; *Era*, February 1, 1896.

58 *Wheeling Register*, July 29, 1893; *Auburn Bulletin*, July/August 1893, 6; *Lewiston Evening Journal*, July 31, 1893, 2.

59 Clara Beckwith, *In the Swim, Autobiography of Miss Clara Beckwith, The World's Champion Lady Swimmer. The Theory and Practice of Swimming Explained and Illustrated by the Modern Mermaid* (Baltimore, Wm. U. Day Printing Co. 1893). No page numbers; *Wheeling Register*, July 29, 1893; *Auburn Bulletin* July/August 1893, 6; *Lewiston Evening Journal*, July 31, 1893, 2.

60 *Sun*, March 26, 1899, 9; March 29, 1899, 7; *Era*, April 15, 1899; Dictionary of Canadian Biography Online 1901-1910 (Volume XIII) I. I. Mayba 2000 University of Toronto/ Université Laval (afn,1154-6S5). Father, Joshua Manning Sabean (afn, 114X-7D2). Mother, Abigail Jane Wade (afn, 114X-7F8). Spouse, S. W. McInnis Hon. (afn, 1154-6RX); Perkins, *The Romance of Old Annapolis Royal*.

61 The Library and Archives Canada. Census of Canada 1901. Brandon City, Brandon, Manitoba, Page#2; Family No.19; Marriage details for Clement Miller. Groom's Father - John C Miller, Saloon/Hotel Keeper, born Hannover, Germany, circa 1836; Mother - Henrietta E. Vogel, born Saxony, Germany, circa 1838. Bride's Father - Manning Beckwith, Mother - Abbie J Wade. Bride's Marital Status –Widowed; 1910 Census.

62 Beckwith, *In the Swim*, no page numbers

63 *Wheeling Register*, July 29, 1893; *Auburn Bulletin* July/August 1893, 6; *Lewiston Evening Journal*, July 31, 1893, 2.

64 Beckwith, *In the Swim*, no page numbers.

65 Census 1870 and 1880; *Boston Daily Globe*, July 28, 1889, 10; *New York Clipper*, April 6, 1880/1890, 56.

66 *Saint Paul Daily Globe*, June 11, 1893, 12; June 25, 1893, 13; July 2, 1893, 8; *Chicago Daily Tribune*, April 1, 1894, 25-26; April 8, 1894, 26; July 15, 1894, 27; September 3, 1894, 6.

67 *San Francisco Call*, April 5, 1895, 13; April 6, 1895, 14; April 7, 1895, 14; April 16, 1895, 8; April 21, 1895, 22.

68 *New York Clipper*, May 19, 1920, 15; *New York Clipper*, May 18, 1895, 173; Rives, 'Beulah Meyer gets a kick out of life'.

69 *New York Clipper*, May 23, 1895/6, 194; September 28, 1895, 469; *Chicago Daily Tribune*, November 23, 1896, 3; *Boston Daily Globe*, November 28, 1897, 30; *New York Clipper*, May 1, 1898, 136; September 11, 1898, 456; November 27, 1898, 645.

70 John M. Olinskey et al. *The Illustrated History of Fairmount Park*, www.oldfairmountpark.com; *Kansas City Journal*, June 16, 1899, 10; June 19, 1899; June 23, 1899, 10; June 20, 1899,11; June 25, 1899, 17; June 28, 1899, 5; July 2, 1899, 16.

71 *Sandusky Star*, July 13, 1899; July 14, 1899; *Star*, July 17, 1899; July 21, 1899.
72 *Buffalo Express*, August 9, 1901; September 22, 1901; *Syracuse Journal*, July 20, 1901, 3.
73 Pan-American Exposition at Buffalo in the State of New York from May 1 to November 1, 1901 http://panam1901.org/documents/panamwomen/corabeckwith.htm; *Daily Public Ledger*, June 15, 1904, 2.
74 *Police Gazette*, June 25, 1904, 2; *Elyria Chronicle*, July 20, 1904; July 21, 1904; *Elyria Reporter* July 27, 1904.
75 *Perrysburg Journal*, August 1, 1902; *Times Democrat*, August 2, 1902; *Ohio Democrat*, April 23, 1903; *Poughkeepsie Daily Eagle*, November 2, 1903; *Morning Star*, February 5, 1904, 4; February 8, 1904, 5; *Daily Public Ledger*, June 15, 1904, 2.
76 *New York Clipper*, June 8, 1901, 319; *Manitoba Free Press*, January 6, 1917, 14.
77 Death Certificate Index - Dubuque County (1917-1926) Page 142. Rosenthal, Cora Beckwith Born 16 Sept. 1870 Maine Died 09 Feb. 1924 Dubuque Mother's Maiden Name - Tyler 031-1461 D2158.
78 *Chicago Daily Tribune* Apr 1, 1894 pp. 25-26; April 8, 1894, 26; July 15, 1894, 27; September 3, 1894, 6; *San Francisco Call* 5 April 1895, 13; 6 April 1895, 14; 7 April 1895, 14; 16 April 1895, 8; 21 April 1895, 22; *Omaha Daily Bee*, 9 August 1899, 2; 13 August 1899, 8; 18 August 1899, 2; 19 August 1899, 5; Olinskey, *The Illustrated History of Fairmount Park*.
79 *The Denver Sunday Post*, July 15, 1900, p.12; *Sandusky Star* Ohio 14 July 1899; *Syracuse Journal*, 20 July 1901, 3; *Daily Public Ledger*, 15 June 1904, 2; *Evening Telegram*, 16 August 1906, 4.
80 *Omaha Daily Bee*, August 9, 1899, 2; August 13, 1899, 8; August 18, 1899, 2; August 19, 1899, 5.
81 Rives, 'Beulah Meyer gets a kick out of life'; *Chicago Daily Tribune* April 1, 1894, 25-26; April, 8, 1894, 26; July 15, 1894, 27; September 3, 1894, 6; *San Francisco Call*, April 5, 1895, 13; April 6, 1895, 14; April 7, 1895, 14; April 16, 1895, 8; April 21, 1895, 22; Olinskey, *The Illustrated History of Fairmount Park*; *Sandusky Star*, July 14, 1899; *Ohio Democrat*, April 23, 1903; *Omaha Daily Bee*, August 9, 1899, 2; August 13, 1899, 8; August 18, 1899, 2; August 19, 1899, 5; *St. Paul Globe*, July 21, 1901, 4; *Minneapolis Journal*, July 20, 1901, 3; *Daily News*, July 20, 1901; *Syracuse Journal*, July 20, 1901, 3.
82 *Daily Public Ledger*, 15 June 1904, 2; *San Francisco Call*, April 6, 1895, 14; *Buffalo Express*, July 12, 1901; August 9, 1901.

83 *Minneapolis Journal*, 20 July 1901, 3; *Daily News* 20 July 1901; *Syracuse Journal*, 20 July 1901, 3.
84 *Daily Express*, 16 August 1901, 5; *Singapore Free Press and Merchantile Advertiser*, 10 September 1901, 3; *Sydney Morning Herald*, 27 September 1901, 4.
85 *St. Paul Globe*, July 21, 1901, 4; *Chicago Daily Tribune*, August 5, 1901, 6; *The Times* (Richmond VA), August 7, 1901, 5; *The Sun*, August 19, 1901.
86 *Buffalo Express*, July 31, 1902; *Ohio Democrat*, April 30, 1903; *Washington Times*, August 26, 1904, 5; *Telegram*, August 26, 1904, 11.
87 *Niagara Falls Gazette*, August 26, 1904; *Urbana Daily Courier*, August 28, 1912, 4; *Manitoba Free Press*, January 6, 1917, 14.
88 *Boston Herald,* September 11, 1889, 3/8?
89 John Bale, 'Ernst Jokl and Layers of Truth', in *Sporting Lives*, ed. Dave Day (Manchester: MMU IPR Publication, 2011), 1-15.
90 Beckwith, *In the Swim*, no page numbers provided; *Wheeling Register*, July 29, 1893; *Auburn Bulletin* July/August, 1893, 6; *Lewiston Evening Journal*, July 31, 1893, 2.
91 *Quincy Daily Journal*, May 23, 1907, 1; *New York Clipper*, September 21, 1912; May 23, 1895/6, 194; *San Francisco Call*, April 5, 1895, 13; April 6, 1895, 14; April 7, 1895, 14; April 16, 1895, 8; April 21, 1895, 22.
92 *Kansas City Journal*, June 16, 1899, 10; June 19, 1899; June 23, 1899, 10; June 20, 1899, 11; June 25, 1899, 17; June 28, 1899, 5; July 2, 1899, 16; *Omaha Daily Bee*, August 9, 1899, 2; August 13, 1899, 8; August 18, 1899, 2; August 19, 1899, 5; *Ohio Democrat*, April 23, 1903; *Police Gazette*, June 25, 1904, 2; *New York Clipper,* April 2, 1906, 270; April 27, 1907, 278; October 21, 1911, 8; *Austin Daily Herald*, September 24, 1907; *Urbana Daily Courier*, August 28, 1912, 4; *Iowa City Citizen*, August 19, 1908, 8.

www.ingramcontent.com/pod-product-compliance
Lightning Source LLC
Chambersburg PA
CBHW071811080526
44589CB00012B/759